PASSING THE LEADERSHIP BATON

"Transition may be the ultimate litmus test of a leader's skill and heart. Tom Mullins is someone who is running the race and has successfully handed off the baton . . . which seems to be rare in the world of ministry. This book will help EVERY leader leave well and effectively pave the way for their successor. Tom collects great wisdom and learnings from others who have walked the road of transition . . . but most important, he shares honestly about his own personal journey with transition and provides tons of practical coaching. Save yourself and the people around you a lot of PAIN . . . read this book!!"

—LANCE WITT, Founder of Replenish Ministries

"Tom Mullins has built one of the great influential churches in America, and he understands local churches from the inside and outside. He has successfully passed the leadership baton to his son Todd, and the work continues to go forward. Any church that is contemplating passing the leadership baton should study this book carefully because Tom Mullins is giving them mature wisdom."

—ELMER TOWNS, Cofounder, Liberty University, Lynchburg, VA

"Coach Tom Mullins tackles one of the greatest challenges facing the Church today. In a time of unprecedented change, churches, educational institutions, and ministries will either fail or succeed in those moments when leadership transition is needed. As leaders of a global ministry based in South Florida, we have not been casual observers of what has happened at Christ Fellowship as Tom and the leadership passed the reins to Todd. Having seen several megachurches and ministries implode during their transitions, we prayed that this 'passing of the baton' would be what those who knew Tom and Todd were believing for.

"What a joy to see that Christ Fellowship has not only survived but thrived since the transition. This stimulating read provides not an aspirational theory, but a practical and proven framework for leadership transition. For years publishers, leaders, and donors have asked us to write a book on how we transitioned the leadership of OneHope. I'm happy to announce that we will never have to write that book because Tom Mullins has written this manifesto for all of us."

—BOB and ROB HOSKINS, Founder and CEO of OneHope

"Tom and Todd Mullins are modeling what is happening at this moment: *Elijah is passing the torch to Elisha*. Having been through this process myself three years ago, I can tell you that the way in which the Mullinses have handled it has been exemplary. Having trouble finding your Elisha? Having trouble becoming 'Barnabas' after the transition? This is the book to not only answer your questions but to inspire you about the joys, challenges, and legacy of transition."

—LARRY STOCKSTILL, Pastor Emeritus, Bethany Church, Baton Rouge, LA

"I've read plenty of books that talk about finishing well, but leading isn't just about reaching our own personal finish line. Part of leading is preparing our organizations and churches to flourish long after we are gone. Letting go is hard, but we have a responsibility to plan for the transition to the next generation, and Tom's book can help us in that process."

—GREG SURRATT, Senior Pastor Seacoast Church, and Author of *Ir-Rev-Rend*

"Tom Mullins is such an inspiration. His ability to motivate, lead, and challenge is grounded in his integrity and serves as a standard for all of us. Now Dr. Mullins offers field-tested, pastoral counsel for those in the vulnerable and often turbulent season of transition. Reading *Passing the Leadership Baton* and implementing its counsel can help you navigate around years of regret."

—JONATHAN SHIBLEY, President, Global Advance; and
DAVID SHIBLEY, Founder and World Representative, Global Advance

"Tom has mastered the elements necessary to successfully transfer the mantle of leadership from one generation to the next, which must be the goal of every leader. The insights he shares in *Passing the Leadership Baton* make the difference in every healthy transition, and I've personally seen these principles implemented at Christ Fellowship. Every leader needs this book."

—DAVID BARTON, Founder and President, WallBuilders

"My friend Tom Mullins hits the nail on the head in his book, *Passing the Leadership Baton*. His strategic mind teaches others what he has spent a lifetime learning. Once again, he serves as a coach to help leaders effectively transition out of one role and posture the organization to succeed going forward! This is a practical guide to creating a legacy of greatness!"

—BISHOP DALE C. BRONNER, DMin, author of *Passing the Baton*, and Founder/
Senior Pastor, Word of Faith Cathedral, Atlanta, GA

"Whether you are leading a ministry or running a corporation, Tom's principles in *Passing the Leadership Baton* are going to help you make leadership transitions at the right time and with the right perspective. It's a must read for any executive."

—ED BASTIAN, President, Delta Air Lines

"We can't think of a better pair to discuss the transition of leadership from one generation to another than Tom and Todd Mullins. We have watched with interest as they have planned, prepared, and successfully transitioned leadership in what appeared to be a seamless exchange of the leadership baton. Their thoughtful preparation and execution is something that we want to learn from and apply in our own transition exchange. The book and their lives are a relational model for all to follow. All we can say is thank you, Tom and Todd!"

—TOM and TODD LANE, Gateway Church

"Many churches and organizations struggle because they fail to prepare for the future. Tom "Mullins has a passion to keep that from happening. More important, he himself has navigated his way through a leadership transition. Tom successfully passed the baton and saw his church grow even stronger through the process. By being intentional, with good direction and wisdom, churches and organizations can navigate through a transition and grow numerically and spiritually through the process."

—DAVE STONE, Pastor, Southeast Christian Church, Louisville, KY

"Leadership transitions are common and uncomfortable. I've had a front row seat as Tom handed off point leadership to Todd. I'm in awe of their gold medal baton pass. Tom's coaching will rescue leaders from unspoken and unplanned conversations that would otherwise cost you the race. This is a gift to leaders."

—KEVIN MYERS, Founding pastor of 12Stone Church, Atlanta, GA

"I once heard Chuck Swindoll make this statement: 'When God's man dies, God's work never does!' That's a great truth about God's providence and His power. However, there is also great truth in this statement from the Bible that says, 'Moreover it is required in stewards that one be found faithful' (1 Cor. 4:2). In both statements, we find truth. God's work never stops but we as workers in the Kingdom must be found faithful in passing the torch to the next generation. Transitions are always difficult and require careful planning and much prayer. My friend, Tom Mullins, has done a masterful job in transitioning a great church to the next generation without missing a beat. And in this book, *Passing the Leadership Baton*, he has given us all great insight so we might learn from him, and others, on how we can do the same. I encourage you to read this book, take notes, and pray over the truths found within. Realize that unless Christ returns first, you will one day have to pass the baton to another generation to continue the work God has called you to do. Be sure to pass the baton in the right way. This book will help you to be found faithful."

—JONATHAN FALWELL, Pastor, Thomas Road Baptist Church, Lynchburg, VA

"Even though my father and I had spent years working with Liberty University trustees to plan for the transition in leadership that would follow his death, it was still a challenging time when my father suddenly died without warning. This book would have been a great help to me during those difficult days. Don't overlook the importance of planning for a transition—whether expected or not. Preparing for your own succession is the hallmark of a great leader. Tom has led the charge on this discussion and his principles in this book will help your organization prepare for the inevitable transitions we will all face."

—JERRY FALWELL, President, Liberty University

PASSING THE **LEADERSHIP** BATON

A Winning Transition Plan for Your Ministry

Tom Mullins

THOMAS NELSON
Since 1798

NASHVILLE   MEXICO CITY   RIO DE JANEIRO

Published in Nashville, Tennessee, by Thomas Nelson. Thomas Nelson is a registered trademark of HarperCollins Christian Publishing.

Published in association with the literary agency of Mark Sweeney & Associates, Bonita Springs, Florida 34135

Thomas Nelson titles may be purchased in bulk for educational, business, fund-raising, or sales promotional use. For information, please e-mail SpecialMarkets@ThomasNelson.com

Library of Congress Control Number: 2014946314

ISBN: 978-0-7180-3119-0 (hardcover)
ISBN: 978-0-7180-3120-6 (e-book)

To my family, who has not only helped me carry the baton, but has helped me pass it well.

Donna, Noelle, Todd, Julie, Jefferson, and Mother, I honor you and love you.

My prayer is that you will keep running the race marked out for you, and that you will finish strong.

About Leadership ✕ Network

Leadership Network fosters innovation movements that activate the church to greater impact. We help shape the conversations and practices of pacesetter churches in North America and around the world. The Leadership Network mind-set identifies church leaders with forward-thinking ideas—and helps them to catalyze those ideas resulting in movements that shape the church.

Together with HarperCollins Christian Publishing, the biggest name in Christian books, the NEXT imprint of Leadership Network moves ideas to implementation for leaders to take their ideas to form, substance, and reality. Placed in the hands of other church leaders, that reality begins spreading from one leader to the next . . . and to the next . . . and to the next, where that idea begins to flourish into a full-grown movement that creates a real, tangible impact in the world around it.

**NEXT: A Leadership Network Resource
committed to helping you grow your next idea.**

leadnet.org/NEXT

《 CONTENTS 》

ACKNOWLEDGMENTS

Thank you to my wife, Donna, for being my life partner. She has faithfully walked beside me down every road our Lord has marked out for us. And her tender humility and commitment have refined and strengthened me during the transitions of life. I am forever grateful for her love.

Thank you to my son, Todd; my daughter Noelle; my daughter Julie; my grandson Jefferson; and my mother. My family has consistently supported me in all the seasons of transition we've walked through together. I wouldn't want to run this race without them.

Thank you to my friend John C. Maxwell. Not only has he been a great friend and a faithful partner in ministry, but he encouraged me to write this book to help the church. His counsel and coaching have been tremendous assets in my life.

Thank you to my assistant, Carolyn Master, for helping me make this project a reality. This book wouldn't be what it is without her help.

Thank you to Charlie and Stephanie Wetzel for their invaluable consultation and guidance on the manuscript.

Thank you to each person who took the time to share his transition story with me. This book is richer because of your input.

Thank you to my Christ Fellowship family. Your grace, faithfulness, and confidence during our transition is the greatest testimony of the principles shared in this book.

FOREWORD

By John C. Maxwell

Tom Mullins and I have known each other for nearly twenty years. He is a dear brother in Christ and one of my closest friends. I love him, Donna, and their whole family. But that's not why I'm writing this foreword to his book. I'm writing it because he succeeded in planning and completing one of the smoothest and most effective church transitions I've ever seen.

Transitions in any kind of organization are important. Many business leaders seem to understand this intuitively. The best corporations have succession plans in place and their leaders spend a great deal of time grooming successors and planning the handoff. Fewer church leaders seem willing to tackle succession planning. Some are afraid to tackle the difficult subject. Others seem to think it's not spiritual to plan ahead. But Jesus had a succession plan, so why shouldn't we?

No doubt, transitions are difficult. One of the toughest things any leader can do is hand off the baton of leadership to another leader of the organization. It takes planning and forethought. It takes dedication to prepare the next leader. It requires a high degree of influence and leadership skill to facilitate the exchange. And it's necessary for outgoing leaders to keep their egos in check while letting go of one of the things they love most.

Tom succeeded in doing this, and I had a front-row seat to watch the whole process, since Tom occasionally asked my advice. I often call Tom the Pied Piper. Everybody loves him and wants to follow him. He could have remained the leader of Christ Fellowship until he died. Few people would have blamed him. He planted the church and nurtured it to become one of the finest and most influential churches in the nation. But Tom didn't do that. He looked to the future and started planning a transition while he was still at the top of his game. And he successfully handed the baton to his son Todd. Today the church is thriving!

I believe you can learn from Tom. No matter whether you're a pastor who recognizes the importance of planning a future transition, the recognized successor wondering how you should go about preparing yourself, or a lay leader who is helping to facilitate a transition process in the church (whether expected or unanticipated), you can find invaluable insight and practical direction in this book.

The true measure of success for a leader is measured by succession. If you love the Church, and want your local church to continue to thrive after a change in leadership, then learn the lessons Tom has to offer. They will help you to transition well.

THE EXCHANGE ZONE

Leading Through Transition

God has given us two hands—one to receive
with and the other to give with.

—BILLY GRAHAM[1]

love the Olympics. I mean, I really love them. I'll even go so
far as to admit that I'm an Olympic junkie. I can't get enough
when they are on television. I stay up until all hours of the night
and keep a TV on in my office to make sure I don't miss out on
anything. It's pitiful how much time I spend watching, but I absolutely love seeing the best athletes in the world competing against
one another, and I love rooting for my country!

I competed in track and field in high school before deciding
to concentrate on football while in college, so I am most excited
when Olympic track and field events are taking place. I'm sure you
can imagine how thrilled I was to have the privilege of attending
the 1996 Summer Games in Atlanta and watching US track and
field Hall of Famer Michael Johnson win the 200- and 400-meter

races with record-setting performances. It was one of the greatest sporting events I've ever witnessed.

Those short sprint races that recognize the fastest men and women in the world are amazing, but the meticulous and calculated partnership between runners in relay races also keeps me riveted. It inspires me to see each runner running his best in his leg of the race and then making a flawless exchange of the baton to the runner who follows him.

At the 1996 games, the US men's 4x100 relay finished second to Canada, but the women's team won the gold. Fortunately, for the men's 4x400 relay, Michael Johnson ran anchor for the team, and the American men brought home the gold in that race.

When you look at the statistics, United States relay teams are unmatched in their success. According to *New York Times* sports reporter Sam Borden, "Since 1932, American women have won as many Olympic gold medals in the 4x100 relay (nine) as all other countries combined. Since 1920, the American men's relay team has won gold at 15 of the 21 Olympics held, with one of the six misses coming because of the 1980 United States boycott of the Moscow Games."[2]

Borden went on to say, "A fluid exchange can make the difference between a successful race and disappointment. On a good pass, the baton spends about 1.8 seconds in the zone. . . . A bad pass might have the baton there for 2.0 seconds. . . . Poor passing can cost a team half a second or more—an eternity in a sport where finishes are often decided by hundredths of a second."[3]

In high school, I ran every relay in which our track team participated. I know from experience that the key to victory in relay races is found in how well the runners pass the baton to their teammates. In every race, there are three exchanges, and each exchange must take place inside a 20-meter passing zone. Getting the baton safely from runner to runner within those exchange zones is the most crucial aspect of a relay.

And along with passing quickly within the zone, it is equally important that runners do everything possible to avoid disqualification. A team is automatically disqualified when a runner goes outside his or her lane or when a pass takes place outside the exchange area. Runners are also disqualified if the baton is dropped during the exchange.

Runners will obviously do whatever they can to keep that baton from falling to the ground, but if you've watched your share of Olympic relay races, as I have, you know it unfortunately does happen, including in the 2008 Beijing Olympics, when the US men's 4x100 relay team dropped the baton during the preliminaries.

I remember that dreadful moment all too well. I was sitting on my couch with my family, feeling so confident that the US team was a sure bet. Rodney Martin took his mark on the starting block. The gun rang out and Rodney leapt ahead of the competition. He rounded the track and made a smooth exchange with Travis Padgett, who raced around to hand the baton off to Darvis Patton. I held my breath for the entire half a minute it took for the first three runners to make their way around the track. Patton entered the final exchange zone as we all slid to the edge of our seats in anticipation of a first-place seed for the finals. But as Patton attempted to hand the baton to Tyson Gay, it somehow slipped from between their grasps and fell to the ground, the sound of its *ting*ing along the track reverberating throughout the arena. Medal hopes for the United States were gone in a flash.

That same day, the US women's 4x100 team lined up for the preliminaries with hopes of redemption for the United States. They, too, had a long history of victory and were favored to move on to the finals and take home the gold. Both Angela Williams and Mechelle Lewis made their runs and transitions flawlessly. But disaster struck once again when Torri Edwards tried to pass the baton to the team anchor, Lauryn Williams. The United States dropped the baton again. No one had expected either the men's or the women's team to lose in the preliminaries; it was inconceivable that it could happen to both on the same day. Everything was over in an instant, and every commentator said the same thing: the race is won and lost in the exchange zone.

CHURCHES ALSO HAVE AN EXCHANGE ZONE

A good pass of the baton of leadership is as crucial to any organization as it is in track and field relays. According to statistics presented at a Leadership Network Succession Conference on March 26, 2013, close to sixty thousand churches go through transitions in leadership each year. Many in my generation who founded churches thirty to forty years ago are now standing at the crossroads of transition. Successfully handing off the leadership baton to a successor is essential if we want our organizations to thrive in the years following our own investment. It requires meticulous planning and the right timing to ensure a smooth and seamless handoff in the exchange zone.

If we think of our own leadership as one leg in the long race ahead for our organization, it's easy to see the need to plan for transitions between us and those who will follow. Inevitably, a handoff will need to be made! And the more prepared we are for the future, the less of a surprise it will be when it's time to make a change. Everyone needs to be thinking about this passing of the baton, but the more I talk to men and women in prominent positions of leadership, the more I realize how few have planned for transition.

My friend Lance Witt and I were talking about this recently, and he remarked that transition planning seems like a fairly new discussion to many of the pastors he coaches through his ministry, Replenish. He said most don't think about it until they are faced with a situation where they have no choice but to make a change—perhaps because the organization is headed in a new direction or because they have outgrown their post. Very quickly, they find that they don't really know where to begin, so they need a coach like Lance to help them through the transition process.

> LIFE IS ONE BIG TRANSITION AFTER ANOTHER.

Life is one big transition after another, and we need to be prepared to shift and adjust as needed. Unfortunately, because many leaders fail to think through the importance of planning for transitions, the outcomes can be devastating, not only for the leaders, but also for the organizations they lead. If you hire the wrong person or fail to prepare that individual adequately to take over his or her new role, the result can be catastrophic. And if you neglect to make sure the organization is strong and able to weather the changes needed to make a successful exchange, those costs can be high too. A poor baton pass can cost you everything.

Robert H. Schuller began preaching in 1955, standing on top of the concession stand at a drive-in theater. By 1970 he had launched his television program, *Hour of Power*, which at its peak had 1.3 million viewers in 156 countries.[4] In 1980 he opened the famous Crystal Cathedral in Southern California. He served there as senior pastor for the next twenty-six years, until he passed the ministry to his son, Robert A. Schuller, in 2006.

The father-son duo had been in ministry together since 1976, when Robert A. began serving on his father's staff. The plan for him to succeed his father had been in motion for the better part of thirty years. Unfortunately, though, the transition was short-lived. In 2008, only two years after the baton had been passed to Robert A., Robert H. announced that he was removing his son as the senior pastor and severely limiting his responsibilities at both the church and the television ministry, due to differences in direction and vision. He said, "For this lack of shared vision and the jeopardy in which this is placing this entire ministry, it has become necessary for Robert and me to part ways."[5]

When Robert A. was asked what he believed ultimately caused the failed transition between his father and him, he pointed to two issues. The first was that Robert H. never really took his hand off the ministry enough to allow him the space to lead. Robert A. believed that, for his dad, stepping away from a ministry that he had built and overseen for a quarter century was simply counterintuitive to everything he knew to do as a leader. As a result, Robert H. couldn't embrace the changes that his son was proposing. They also apparently never had a formal agreement about their transition roles and responsibilities. I think they believed that because they had worked together for so long, they would be fine in this new season. They were dead wrong.

The second issue Robert A. believed contributed to his dismissal was sibling squabbles. He believed that the fact that his three sisters were not encouraged to be ordained to take over the church, along with the fact that it was quite rare for the leadership of megachurches to be handed over to women, caused a lot of bitterness.[6] Without official ordination, they were not able to take on senior leadership roles. Robert A. believed that this led them to stir up dissension, and in fact, they did cause their father to question Robert A.'s leadership and ultimately demand that he step down.

After one of the daughters got ordained and took over senior leadership, the financial stability of the ministry continued to steadily deteriorate. Membership declined dramatically with all the unsettling changes, the church board lost confidence in the family's ability to work through their differences, and soon, everything started falling apart.

The Schuller family and their ministries were on a path to failure. In just a few short years the board dismissed all Schuller family members from leadership positions on staff and on the board. They tried to rebound from all the problems that came from the transition, but unfortunately, nothing helped. The Crystal Cathedral finally had to file for bankruptcy. The reputation of one of the best-known megachurches in America had sadly been reduced to inter-familial squabbles, mounds of debt, and For Sale signs. The church was eventually sold to the Roman Catholic Diocese to help pay off the debts it had accrued in its latter years of ministry.

Today, the Schuller family is slowly rebuilding. Each member is pursuing individual ministry endeavors; and it appears that forgiveness and love are leading them as they work through their differences.

I truly believe so many of the issues the Schullers encountered could have been avoided if they had spent more time strategically planning for their transition. I think they left a lot unsaid as the time neared for Robert H. to step down. If they had addressed some of the concerns and questions head-on, perhaps they would have been able to work through the family issues more objectively. Maybe they also would have been able to anticipate some of the leadership differences so they could deal with them before the transition took place as well.

ANOTHER KIND OF HANDOFF

Like Robert H. Schuller, I too was blessed to have my son ministering at my side from nearly the beginning. My wife, Donna, and I started Christ Fellowship in our home in 1984 with about five families, who soon grew to forty people. Our son, Todd, and daughter, Noelle, were fully invested and actively involved in the growth and development of the church from day one because we were committed to a life in ministry as a family.

The church continued to grow, so we moved from our home to a nearby elementary schoolhouse where we cleaned peanut butter and jelly off cafeteria tables dutifully each week before holding services. We focused our ministry on loving God and loving people the best we knew how. As a church, we began regular outreach to the area nursing home and cared for the less fortunate in our community whenever we could. We simply looked for opportunities to express the love of God in practical ways. And as a family, we had a revolving door of people in need of a place to stay or a meal to eat. We just wanted to be faithful to whatever God asked of us, and all along the way, we prayed earnestly for God to expand our reach.

When we outgrew the schoolhouse, Todd found an old riding barn down the road that we were able to purchase and convert into a sanctuary with the help of our founding families. Each family sacrificed tremendously—taking out second mortgages, cashing out retirement funds, and giving their most precious possessions to expand our impact for the cause of Christ.

I truly believe that our unity and devotion to God's mission to reach this region is what He used to help us grow tremendously once we got into that building in 1992, which we now refer to as our Gardens South Campus. The first weekend we held services in our new building, we had 326 attendees. From that time on, we steadily grew to the point that we were running five services a weekend just to accommodate the four thousand people who were pulling into our parking lot! Traffic was often backed up so far that some people just came to see what the fuss was all about. The miracles came when they actually returned and gave their hearts to the Lord. It was a dynamic season of growth for our church as we watched people's lives being changed for eternity.

It wasn't long before we realized we would need to start praying about buying land to build a larger building. There was no way we could continue to grow at that speed and not outgrow our existing facility on four and a half acres. As it was, I was barely managing the toll of five services along with caring for a now huge church family with the help of a very small paid staff. We knew God had more in store and we desperately needed Him to come through in a big way.

As we prayed for clarity on what was next, Bill Groot, a man who owned forty acres of land directly across the street from our existing property, came to see me. As he entered my office I saw a roll of papers tucked under his arm. He flopped the papers down on my desk and slid them toward me. Then he pointed to the cash offer of $4 million from a developer for his land. I looked back up at him and said, "Bill, you can't take that offer. You and I both know that land is being saved for the Lord's work. You have to tell them no and sell us the land instead."

Even before that moment, I had been convinced that Christ Fellowship would eventually buy that land from Bill to build our new building. I used to attend cattle auctions with Bill just to get to know him. We eventually discussed the option for us to purchase his land, but he and I both knew that Christ Fellowship was in no position to buy it at that point because we had no financial reserves; everything we received went to underwrite the ministries of the church and to missions.

After we talked about it at length, he walked out of my office that day agreeing not only to refuse the developer's offer, but also to carry the mortgage note on the land until we were able to pay him for it. He generously passed up a full cash offer to hold that land for us and even ended up leaving $1 million of the $4 million we had agreed to pay him to the church in his will.

It was 2000 when we moved into our Gardens North Campus, which allowed us to greatly expand our ministry programs while providing us with the space we needed to accommodate our ever-growing church family.

In 1993, at the same time we were building our North Campus, Donna and I took a mission trip to Romania and Russia, where we toured several orphanages and saw the deplorable conditions of the refugee children left in their care. It absolutely broke our hearts, and we returned with a clear calling to do something to help children in need in our own community, so during a prayer service Donna wept and pleaded with God to open doors for us to somehow make a difference. That night I announced to our church family that we would be intentional about living out God's message from Isaiah 1:17: "Seek justice, encourage the oppressed. Defend the cause of the fatherless" (NIV). Our church family rallied around the vision, and in 2001 we opened the Place of Hope, a faith-based, state-licensed children's welfare organization that provides family-style foster care; maternity care for young, unwed mothers; housing and support services for victims of human trafficking; and state-approved adoption and foster care training and placements.

God was expanding our ministry by leaps and bounds. We were growing in so many ways. In fact, in a matter of months after moving into our Gardens North Campus, we had doubled from four thousand people to eight thousand, and we were back to holding five services again! That continued growth forced us to closely consider the long-term effectiveness of our model for ministry at the church. We had to ask ourselves how we could realistically continue to grow in our existing space when there was no more land to purchase in that location! We also had to consider the fact that we had a large number of families traveling as far as forty-five miles to come to and from church each weekend. As we prayed and researched, we knew we had to expand and extend our reach. We needed to take the church to the people. We would be going to a multisite model.

We started our first new campus in Royal Palm Beach in 2004, which is about thirty minutes from our Gardens campus. Then, expanding the vision to reach the heart of the city for Christ, we began meeting at the Harriet Himmel Theater at CityPlace in downtown West Palm Beach in 2005. We started having services to reach the large Latin American community in our area. And in 2008, we launched an online campus where twenty-five thousand people currently worship together weekly. That same year, we opened a campus in Stuart, and have since purchased 321 acres to build a permanent facility there.

God has done a mighty work through Christ Fellowship over the last thirty years! And through all those years of growth and expansion, Todd was at my right hand, serving in whatever capacity was needed. In the early years he served as our worship leader, youth pastor, secretary, and custodian. As Christ Fellowship grew up as a church, Todd grew up as a leader. He had a clear calling to lifelong leadership at Christ Fellowship, so I knew he would one day be my successor.

In 2011 we completed the transition from my leadership to Todd's—a few short years after our twenty-fifth anniversary as a church. Before we exchanged the baton of leadership, I put together and implemented a five-year plan to prepare Todd to officially take over as lead pastor. It was one of the most gratifying and successful things I've been a part of in ministry. Since Todd has taken over, we have experienced exponential growth and have expanded our impact beyond anything we had experienced in the past.

In 2012 we bought an old Dillard's store in the Boynton Beach Mall that we renovated to serve as another permanent location. In 2013 we took over a church in Okeechobee, Florida, to start a campus there. And we also recently opened a campus in New York City. We currently have more than twenty-five thousand people meeting on our regional campuses and twenty-five thousand more joining us in our online campus each week.

EVERY LEADER AND EVERY CHURCH NEEDS TO EMBRACE TRANSITION PLANNING.

EVERY CHURCH NEEDS A TRANSITION PLAN

I believe every leader and every church needs to embrace transition planning because it's best for the life of the outgoing leader, the success of the successor, and the future of the church. In my assessment, winning transitions are vital for the continued health and growth of the church. However, that reality doesn't minimize how difficult transitions can be.

My friend, leadership expert John C. Maxwell, said our transition at Christ Fellowship was one of the best transitions in leadership he had witnessed, and he encouraged us to record the lessons we've learned so we can help others. Accordingly, the purpose of this book is to coach you to lead well through your own transition. Whether you are the leader of a megachurch, the pastor of a small congregational church, or a board member spearheading a transition, this book is for you. My hope is that the principles and strategies we will share will help you think through, pray about, plan, and execute a successful transition plan.

I will share more of the Christ Fellowship transition story along with insights and stories from a number of other outgoing leaders and successors whom I interviewed. As we head out on this journey together, we will tackle a number of important issues, including:

1. determining the timing for when it's best for a leader to transition out and bring in a new leader;
2. properly preparing for transition, while taking into account how challenging this can be for most leaders;

3. creating an atmosphere receptive to change because transitions have the potential to be taxing on the organization's team and those they lead;
4. putting together a successor selection and preparation process;
5. providing helpful tips solely for successors; and
6. handling crisis-driven transitions, whether from the unexpected death or the moral failure of the predecessor.

LEADERS MUST THINK ABOUT THE UNTHINKABLE

I recently heard about the unexpected deaths of three pastors at Grace Christian Center in Killeen, Texas. The senior pastor of more than thirty years, Terry Whitley, along with his wife and associate pastor, Jan Whitley, and another of their associate pastors, Steve Timmerman, all died when a tire blew on the van in which they were traveling as they returned from a mission trip in Bulgaria.[7] Sadly, their board had no transition plan for such a crisis. As a result, many pastors around the country have come forward to offer support, care, and leadership to their congregation in the wake of such a devastating loss.

Have you ever stopped and asked yourself, "What if something were to happen to me or my senior leader today? Who would preach this weekend? What would the church do? How would we ensure the ongoing health of the church?"? These are sobering questions we don't like to think about, but none of us knows the time the Lord will call us home. Do you have a plan in place if it were to happen today? Are you sure your organization will be secure and cared for in the future?

And even if you have many long years of life ahead, have you and your board planned for your retirement? Do you have a timeline for your transition out of the organization? Are you actively investing in the next generation of leadership in your organization? Do you and your board have a process for selecting a successor?

And heaven forbid that it would occur, but do you have a plan and procedures in place in case there is a moral failure among the leadership of your organization? Do you know how you would handle that situation and what the chain of command would be for your staff? How would you or your team handle the devastation of such a betrayal?

>> A TRANSITION WILL BE ONE OF THE GREATEST TESTS OF YOUR LEADERSHIP, BUT IT WILL ALSO SERVE AS ONE OF THE GREATEST REWARDS AND TESTIMONIES OF YOUR LEGACY.

I'm sure you will agree with me that these are critical questions to consider. If you asked them of yourself and had no solid answers, this book is for you. I truly believe the topics covered here will help you answer those questions with confidence. Our goal is to help equip you and your board to plan for and manage transitions successfully.

We leaders must prepare ourselves, our organizations, and our successors to receive the baton of leadership so that there are even greater days ahead. No doubt, a transition will be one of the greatest tests of your leadership, but it will also serve as one of the greatest rewards and testimonies of your legacy. We only get one chance in the exchange zone. Let's protect the baton and pass it well.

THE BATON IS NOT
YOURS TO KEEP

Keeping the Right Perspective

Almost anything is easier to get into than out of.

—AGNES ALLEN[1]

On July 27, 1999, one of the greatest running backs of all time, Barry Sanders of the Detroit Lions, announced his retirement. He was only thirty-one, still in the prime of his career, and only 1,458 yards shy of the NFL career rushing record. This left many wondering why he would step away when he did.

Do I think his decision was premature? Perhaps. He had been a Heisman Trophy winner at Oklahoma State and had a very impressive career with the Lions, rushing an average of 1,500 yards per season for ten years. He was unstoppable. There is no doubt in my mind that he had the potential for even more success. However, from the interviews and articles I've read and the documentaries I've watched about him over the years, I have to admit there is something to be said for leaving when you are on top of your game.

Think back to our relay race example. A runner is best situated to hand off the baton when he is moving at full speed in the exchange zone. Success in the handoff demands that the runner be at the peak of his stride.

Barry Sanders certainly knew he was at the top of his game and had a lot left to give. But it appears that he had peace because he had sensed his passion was waning. He knew it was time to finish strong and move on.

We need to cultivate that same discernment as we make our transitions in leadership. Sure, you could keep running until your legs give out, but it's important to remember that you will never be the one to carry the baton across the finish line. God has a lot more to do through His people, and each person's individual leg of the race will one day come to an end. There is always someone else ready to run the next leg.

In his book *Transition Plan*, Bob Russell, the former senior pastor of Southeast Christian Church in Louisville, Kentucky, mentioned a minister who had told his congregation as he was resigning, "There are three ways I can leave. You can carry me out, you can kick me out, or I can walk out. I choose to walk out."[2] I think that's a wise way to go! In my opinion, smart leaders always walk out while they are on top of their game because when they are at their zenith, the organization is strong and will be able to withstand the winds of change that come from a transition.

It's important that we prepare ourselves well for that inevitable moment of transition, giving careful thought and consideration to what we want our lives to look like beyond the exchange zone.

The future we want after the transition won't just fall in our laps. We have to plan for it.

PLANNING FOR LIFE BEYOND THE EXCHANGE ZONE

Here are some things you need to think about:

Count the Cost

A transition will always cost you something. Whether through abandoning your comfort zone for the sake of the organization, experiencing the grief over what feels like a loss, or feeling confused over your future plans, you will always pay an emotional price.

> A TRANSITION WILL ALWAYS COST YOU SOMETHING.

I think the significance of this is often overlooked until the outgoing leader is knee-deep in the process and he or she begins struggling to accept the change or navigate through its many dimensions. It can be quite challenging to wrestle with the emotional attachments we feel to the work we've invested in for years. I've talked to a number of guys who have gone through transitions and struggled immensely with the sadness they felt in stepping away. For many, it meant leaving their church or organization entirely so they could make room for the new guy to lead without the added pressure of their presence. For others, it meant sitting in the pews silently and watching someone else cast new vision from what was their platform for so many years. And sadly, for some, it meant watching the demise of the organization due to an inferior leader's inability to lead at the same level.

It's normal to struggle with the emotional side of transitioning out of a life work. In fact, I would even say it should be expected. And the greatest thing you can do to manage those emotions is to plan for and to pray through them.

Back in 1995, John Maxwell transitioned out of the role of senior pastor at Skyline Church in San Diego. So when I was preparing for my transition, I asked him how he had handled the emotional side of leaving a place where he had served for fourteen years. He said he actually made a list of all the things that leaving would cost him. And he quickly discovered that one of the biggest adjustments for him would be losing the relationships he had built with his church family. He knew leaving Skyline meant leaving people, which tugged at his heart.

John also had to accept that his ego wouldn't be fulfilled by the familiarity that pastoring a megachurch afforded him in his community. And as he continued with his companies INJOY and INJOY Stewardship Services, which helped churches with stewardship planning, he had to accept that he might lose his influence with pastors after a few short years because he was no longer a pastor himself.

He even had to accept the reality of leaving Skyline as a level 5 leader and starting over again as a level 1 leader.[3] And of course by resigning his role as a pastor, he wouldn't be preaching on week-ends or seeing the miracles of God's restoration work each week in the lives of the people he loved.

Those are just a few of the realities John had to face, but he was quick to say that the process of writing out the inevitable changes helped him plan for them and manage the emotional soul care he needed to step out and make the transition.[4]

Don't neglect this process yourself. Take the time to really con-sider what a transition will cost you so you can plan ahead for the conflicting feelings you will likely face as you make the transition.

Seek Out a Coach

When I coached football I always sought out other coaches who had won at higher levels than I had. I often went to their coaching clinics and summer camps, hoping to pick up a few new plays and practice drills. I knew they were doing certain things that made them successful, and I wanted to implement these with my team as well.

In a leadership transition, I believe we can only be successful when we lean in to a coach who can guide us to victory. This is also true in the business world, which places high value on career coaches. And the Bible is full of coaching relationships that serve as models for us. I believe that a transition coach can help you see and assess things from a different perspective than you are able to on your own.

One thing coaches do well is prepare. All coaches in sports spend hours each week watching film and working on their game plan for their next opponent. And just as preparation is the key to

victory on the ball field, it is equally vital for any leadership transition. You need a coach who is a meticulous planner and a strategic
thinker because he will help you consider all the necessary steps
you need to take along the way. A coach will also ask you questions and encourage communication. This keeps your preparation
moving forward. Having a coach means that you have someone
else to help oversee the development of your game plan.

Coaches also understand the importance of timing. As you
probably know, calling the right play at the right time is essential
in a ball game. And boy, is that true when you are going through
a transition! You and your coach need to think through the best
time to transition for the health and well-being of the church and
your team. You will need to factor in time for your successor to be
prepared and for any issues to be worked out before he or she takes
over. You need to think about how the timing will affect existing programs and initiatives that are already in motion or about to
begin. Don't plan anything that could put an added pressure on the
new leader to rally donors and support for a significantly new vision.

A coach will assist you in determining the right timing for
your transition by helping you recognize and seize momentum.
Most of us cannot do this without assistance, because we tend
to overlook the fact that the best times for transitions are often
disguised as the most successful times in our ministries. The best
time to step down is when you can point out all the great things
that are happening. This gives your congregation confidence for a
bright future. It also sets your successor up for even greater success. Strong momentum always serves as the wind that carries
your successor into the next leg of the race.

A good coach is also a good recruiter. You need someone on your team who can help you think through the positions you might need to fill in order for you to step out and your successor to step in. A coach can also help you think about who is in a position that might not fit any longer under the new leadership structure.

Over the last year I have been coaching a friend as he prepares to transition out of the senior leadership role of his church. We've been talking lately about determining his successor and whether any of his existing staff members could take on this new role. Interestingly enough, once we determined the right set of responsibilities, gifts, and skills for a successor, it was clear that the person he had his eye on was actually not the right choice. This forced us to spend time realigning his staff so he would have everyone in the right position and be able to invest in other people with potential.

In addition to repositioning existing team members, sometimes when trying to make a healthy transition, it becomes obvious that we don't even have the right people on the team yet. When that is the case, we have to intentionally seek out the right people to add to our team. Good coaches are always scouting and recruiting, and you need someone in your corner doing just that during a transition.

You also need a coach who will help you make adjustments when and where they are needed. In football, a coach only has trends and prior plays to rely on in planning for a game. Sometimes the other team pulls out a play that you weren't expecting, and you need to make a quick adjustment. For this reason, the head coach on the sidelines gets prompts and warnings from the assistant coaches in the sky box throughout the entire game as they see and anticipate things that are simply impossible to see from the sideline. In a transition, there will be times when things don't go as planned and you will have to make a change. A coach will help you see those things and coach you through the options you have to make needed adjustments.

Todd and I were privileged to have John Maxwell, the greatest leadership teacher in the world, as our transition coach. He easily met all of our qualifications. He was able to speak as both an outgoing leader and a successor, since many years before he had succeeded the founding pastor at Skyline. As a dear personal friend and one of our teaching pastors, he is intimately acquainted with the inner workings of Christ Fellowship and with Todd's and my unique relationship as a father-son team. The many conversations we shared were life-giving and affirming for us as we worked our plan.

Having a coach like John who was close to the organization worked well for us, but sometimes it takes an outside, objective coach. My friend Chuck Wall owns Freight Handlers, Inc., one of the country's leading providers of unloading and product handling services. When it was time for Chuck to transition out of the CEO role, he and his son, Ryan, hired an outside consultant to coach them. Ryan said, "Prior to beginning the transition journey, I heard stories of other organizations transitioning based on executives feeling the idea was right and the timing great. In their drive to 'make it happen' they pulled the trigger without an outside perspective. They transitioned and created confusion and a disruption to the culture. Going at it alone is a recipe for unnecessary challenges that will rob from the more important priorities. Utilizing a coach is allowing us to have the wisdom of an outside perspective that can bring a multitude of positives."[5]

Having a coach by your side is an invaluable investment, but if you can't have one, you can still talk to others who have gone through transitions, and also read books on the topic. My wife, Donna, always says, "Books are great mentors." It's true. When Todd and I were approaching our transition, we read *Transition Plan* (see note 2). It affirmed our direction and gave us discussion points for the journey. We also attended a Leadership Network online simulcast called "Succession: Essential Learnings on Healthy Church Leadership Transitions." In it, more than twenty outgoing leaders and successors shared their stories and provided helpful tips for making a successful transition.

> WE ALL NEED A COACH DURING
> A TRANSITION SEASON.

The bottom line is, we all need a coach during a transition season. Try your best to find one. There are some tough and confusing roads leaders must travel down. Let someone run with you so you can make the exchange well.

Decide What's Next

Tom Stoppard said, "Every exit is an entry somewhere else."[6] And John Maxwell put it this way: "Never leave something. Go to something. There's a difference between 'I have to leave it because I'm going *to* something' and 'I have to leave because it's over here, but I have nothing planned.'[7] It's really important to make sure that when you leave your current role, you know what your plans are for the next leg of your personal race.

"Every exit is an entry somewhere else."
—TOM STOPPARD

Knowing what's next will provide you with peace of mind. There are a lot of emotional twists and turns on the transition journey. One thing that really helps alleviate some of that angst is to have a plan for what you will do next. Some guys I've talked to failed to plan for life beyond the exchange zone and found themselves facing depression and financial strains that incapacitated them and sacrificed the great momentum they had when they transitioned out. Planning always provides peace.

Being aware of what's next will also give you a sense of anticipation, knowing you will be investing in something new. If you are a Type A visionary leader like myself, you feel as though you need to be productive at all times.

I knew when I made my transition at sixty-five that I had a lot of life still in me and I couldn't sit around idly. I'm thankful that Todd still has a role for me on his team. I meet with him weekly as his sounding board and confidant. I leverage my years of experience to pour into the emerging generation of leaders at Christ Fellowship. I still help with building acquisitions for our growing campus development, overseas missions projects, stewardship initiatives and campaigns, and speaking on weekends a few times a quarter. I also plan to write more during this season and get out and speak at conferences, military training events, and churches around the country.

This new season also opened up an opportunity for me to step in as the president of EQUIP, John Maxwell's nonprofit organization dedicated to raising up Christian leaders around the world. I had served on the board for many years, and shortly after my transition with Todd, someone was needed to serve in this capacity. As a result, I have been able to help give direction and oversight to the ministry as we embark on new initiatives to develop leaders.

It has been a fulfilling, exciting season for me, but I know it could have been really trying if I hadn't planned for what life would look like after the baton was exchanged. I could never just sit around and wait for life to happen. And frankly, I don't believe in retirement for kingdom saints! There is always some way we can serve in the local church or in God's mission around the world, no matter how old we are.

Establish Your Future Role in the Organization

I mentioned that I'm thankful to still have a role on the Christ Fellowship team. I realize this is fairly unique for most people transitioning out of a senior leadership role in their church or organization. Todd and I have always been a team. He was my right-hand man for about twenty-five years before I handed off the baton. We work well together, so it has been a natural fit for me to stay on and help in any way Todd needs me.

We did have a lot of discussions during our years of planning to determine what areas I would need to step out of completely to let him fulfill the master vision he had received from God for the church. This helped us know exactly what each of us would be doing as we moved forward. And that clarity in our roles also helped the team around us to have clear expectations.

My friend Dr. David Shibley founded Global Advance in 1990 to provide encouragement, resources, and training for pastors in destitute nations of the world. They currently sponsor indigenous training and ministry encouragement for more than half a million frontline shepherds in eighty nations and counting. When his son Jonathan took over the presidency in 2010, the two had long discussions with their board about what David's role would look like moving forward. They, too, came to the conclusion that David still had a role on their team. This included ensuring that the ministry stays strong and biblical in both its theology and missiology, helping to transfuse the passion and urgency of their mission to the next generation of its leadership, being available to counsel the incoming president, and helping to fortify the ministry's financial future by encouraging legacy giving.[8]

As you can see from both of our examples, it *can* work to have the outgoing leader assume a new role, but if you are going to stay on board in some capacity, both of you must be secure and have the roles clearly defined. If the incoming leader needs the space to lead without the former leader looking over his shoulder or worrying about him stepping into areas he needs to own, it's probably not going to work for the former leader to remain on the team. I've always said it's the outgoing leader's baton to give up until he or she feels it's time to make the transition, but it's the successor's baton to run with moving forward. Once you let go of the baton, it's not yours to hold anymore. Don't try to take it back again. You no longer call the shots. You've got to know when it's time to step back or even bow out.

Some thought also needs to go into whether the outgoing leader remains a member of the church. I think this is also a valid discussion to have between the outgoing leader, the successor, and the board. For a lot of outgoing church leaders that I spoke with, they felt they needed to leave completely, making a clean break, so they could give their successors free rein and the confidence to lead without the added pressure of their presence and influence.

When John Maxwell took over at Skyline, he had heard that his predecessor, Pastor Orval Butcher, was going to leave the church and attend services elsewhere because he didn't want to be in the way. John approached Pastor Butcher and told him, "You don't have to do that. You founded this church, and I want you to stay here."[9] John assured him that it would work if they both just agreed to honor each other in front of others. Then John gave Pastor Butcher open-door privileges to come and speak to him anytime Pastor Butcher saw something that concerned him. John simply asked that Pastor Butcher promise to keep the discussions between the two of them. And in kind, John committed to never speak negatively about any choices Pastor Butcher had made while leading the church. This arrangement worked well for them because they elevated each other and kept their unity intact.

Even after having amicable conversations with their successors about staying or going, some outgoing leaders still feel as though they need to cut ties and let the new leader start fresh. There's a lot of wisdom in that decision as well, but never minimize your value to your successor in the weeks and months that follow your departure.

I interviewed Dave Stone, Bob Russell's successor at Southeast Christian Church in Louisville, Kentucky. Bob had felt the right thing to do to secure Dave's success was to leave the church entirely for one year after the baton exchange. Unfortunately, Dave felt as if he was floundering. Even though he had been on Bob's team for seventeen years prior to the transition, he found that the people who had loved and trusted him during that grooming time were now doubting his ability and vision. The congregation dropped from eighteen thousand in attendance to seventeen thousand in the first eighteen months following the transition. The drop in attendance was heartbreaking for Dave, and he struggled immensely with feelings of failure and disappointment.

Bob and Dave had minimal contact during that time, only speaking casually when they ran into each other around town. It wasn't until a year after the transition that Bob invited Dave to play golf and catch up. When Bob asked Dave how he felt things were going, Dave admitted his heartache over the loss of members. He said, "I feel as though I have let you and God down." Bob replied, "You have not let me down! If someone were to tell me when we went through a major transition that we'd only lose one thousand people, I would take that as a huge victory! In a situation where someone like myself had been there for forty years, we should have lost more."[10]

That little bit of perspective helped Dave turn the corner and embrace the journey God had him on at Southeast Christian. In fact, Dave not only grew back the one thousand he lost, but Southeast Christian has continued to grow steadily over the years and expanded to multiple, thriving campuses. Southeast Christian is one of the greatest churches in the nation, and Dave Stone is a tremendous leader. But in retrospect, both he and Bob said that if they had the transition to do again, they would be a lot more intentional to schedule monthly meetings together for that first year. A meeting in those first crucial months might have saved Dave a lot of unnecessary angst.

> ALL SUCCESSORS CRAVE THE
> APPROVAL AND ENCOURAGEMENT
> ONLY A PREDECESSOR CAN OFFER.

I'm convinced that all successors crave the approval and encouragement only a predecessor can offer. If you are the outgoing leader, it's important to realize that you still have a role. Whether it's serving in a new capacity on the team, maintaining your membership at the church with honor, stepping away and providing counsel and encouragement to your successor as he fills his new shoes, or simply praying from a distance, you have a role. Don't leave before you are supposed to. Take time to discuss together what will best serve your successor and be as supportive as you can.

STUMBLING BLOCKS TO TRANSITIONING WELL

Being aware of the things that might inhibit us from making a good exchange is just as important as planning to do the right things during the exchange. Because of this, I would be remiss if I didn't take time in this chapter to discuss some of the common stumbling blocks outgoing leaders have to face head-on. As I've walked the transition road myself and talked to and counseled a number of other ministry leaders doing the same, these seem to be the most common stumbling blocks to avoid along the way.

Ownership: "But this is my baby!"

I think one of the most difficult things for a lot of outgoing leaders is simply stepping away from everything they've built and invested in for a significant number of years. Often, it has become the platform for their credibility as leaders and value as individuals. A change in that role threatens their security and identity.

Founders particularly fall into this category. When you start something, nurture it, and enjoy the privilege of watching it grow, you will naturally feel a sense of loyalty and pride in it. This can make it really hard to step away and leave it in someone else's hands.

It's like watching your child grow up and get married. You know it's a wonderful thing for your kids to leave the nest and start their own families, but your heart still aches a little bit to know they aren't your babies anymore. You can't protect them the way you once did. You can't be the one who makes decisions for them anymore. You can't manage their lives the way you had. They belong to someone else now.

At an even more fundamental level, as an outgoing leader you have to realize that despite the fact that you may have invested a large portion of your life to your ministry, it's not "your" ministry. I'm certain we would all verbally acknowledge that ministry belongs to the Lord, but our response to transition is often an indicator of our understanding and acceptance of that fact.

Being a leader of a congregation makes you a steward of the gifts and talents God has given you. John Maxwell told me, "I have a hard time when pastors refer to the church as '*my* church.' No! It isn't *your* church; it's God's church! Now, don't get me wrong. I do believe pastors should be proud of and love their church. This isn't the same thing. The '*my* church' attitude is a pride issue that causes transition problems, because if I really think it's *my* church, then I will expect the church to serve *my* needs. And when that happens, I become unwilling to transition for the betterment of God's work in *His* church."[11]

Bob and Rob Hoskins of OneHope, an organization working to get God's Word in the hands of every child around the globe, made their transition in 2004 when Bob got sick with stage 4 cancer. When asked whether it was challenging for him to move into a support role, Bob said,

> Some of the problem comes when pride creeps in and people begin to feel like it's theirs and that without them, it's going to fail. . . . It's not yours! If it's yours, it has no eternal future; but if it's God's, then entrust it to Him. . . . Despite the cancer and if Rob hadn't been there ready to take the baton, I would have had to release the leadership to someone else. In my seventy years of

ministry, I've seen some tragic losses for the kingdom because people simply weren't willing to release what God had allowed them to be a part of when their season was over.[12]

It's so important to remember that we are simply stewards of God's work. Having this perspective makes it easier to transition, because we know His master plan for His kingdom is at work. Francis Chan put it well when he said, "The key to everything is surrender."[13] We must simply be willing to do what God wants. Trust His timing, having no personal attachment to anything other than His will. He will help you keep your purpose and platform in perspective as you surrender it to Him daily.

Identity: "But this is what I do!"

Financial advisor Paul Clitheroe said, "For many people a job is more than an income, it's an important part of who we are. So a career transition of any sort is one of the most unsettling experiences you can face in your life." Our identity and association with our career has the potential to be a huge stumbling block. There is no doubt about that.

Lance Witt observed this in men in their mid-sixties who have been serving in ministry for thirty-five to forty years. He said, "They have wrapped their identity up so much in being a pastor of a church that the idea of moving beyond that is very hard."[14] These individuals often don't want to leave, because they don't know who they are outside their role as pastor.

This is why it's so important that you know what you are going to do next. You have to have a focus for life beyond the exchange zone. Take inventory of your gifts, talents, and dreams. What's on the table? Where can you add value next? Assess who you are and the unique calling God has on your life, particularly as it relates to the next leg of your personal race.

I think becoming a football coach prepared me well for my transition in ministry because I experienced even more fulfillment on the sidelines than I had during my years playing on the field. I loved coaching and seeing my guys expertly execute the plays that I had designed to leverage their strengths. Nothing could compare to the joy that came from positively impacting a group of young guys like coaching did.

Those experiences and memories made it so much easier to embrace my role as coach since my transition. Once again I get to experience the joy of a coach when I see my son and the younger guys on our team fulfilling their calling in their generation. It's remarkably satisfying to play a small part in their success now. For me, it was simply a shift in thinking as I made room for others to step up and use their gifts while I coach from the sidelines.

In addition to having a plan and serving as a coach, it would help to focus less on what you *do*, and more about who you *are*—who God has designed you to be. Even if you aren't in the transition zone yet, this is an important concept to embrace. Replace the notion in your head that what you do is the most important thing, with the truth that God has a unique plan for you that far exceeds the circumstances of your employment. He will give you a fresh perspective and a renewed joy if you will just have open hands to accept what He has for you next; but first you must lean in to Him to determine your purpose and identity.

Capacity: "But I'm still alive and kicking!"

As we discussed in our relay example, the timing of transitions is central to their success. Though you may very well feel that you have a lot more you can do, you must prayerfully and thoughtfully consider both the pros and cons to your staying.

Your own sense of comfort and contentment in your role should not be the determining factor in whether you stay longer or not. In fact, I believe very little of your decision should be based on your own feelings about it. Feelings come and go. We've already established that it will be an emotional journey regardless of the timing; that's a given. Your decision needs to be based on when it's best for the organization and for your successor.

Your job throughout the transition period is to determine what's next for you and move toward that new endeavor with the momentum you are carrying from transitioning well. Yes, there is still something for you to do somewhere, but the belief that you still have the energy to fulfill your to-do list at this post isn't reason enough to stay. In fact, your staying could keep the organization from moving forward with some new and innovative methods that could better reach the emerging generation.

My friend Larry Stockstill, the former senior pastor of Bethany World Prayer Center, said, "Elijah had to find Elisha in order for his ministry to release a double portion. Every generation brings new and fresh ideas. The outgoing generation operates on 'dreams' and not 'visions.'"[15] At some point, we all have to pass the baton so God can release new vision and blessing for the next generation of ministry. We outgoing leaders must faithfully fulfill our calling in our time and then be willing to move aside for the new work God wants to do through someone else.

Security: "But I'm not financially ready for this!"

As you craft your transition plan, one thing you will need to spend time thinking about is how you will make money to provide for you and your family after you leave your existing role. This is so important because it gives you financial stability beyond the exchange zone. This will give you peace that you will be taken care of and assure that you go through with the transition at the right time for everyone involved.

I can't tell you how often I have heard of situations in which this was given little to no consideration and it ended up either stalling the outgoing leader's transition or causing bitterness and strife. And in almost every situation, the reasons were the same. Either the outgoing leader hadn't personally planned on the financial ramifications of leaving, or the church hadn't had any formal discussions or agreements about it.

In the first chapter I mentioned the botched transition of Robert H. Schuller, founder of the Crystal Cathedral and the television program *Hour of Power*, and his son Robert A. Schuller. Sadly, Robert H. also ran into a heap of financial issues during his transition, to the point that he and his wife, Arvella, had to file for bankruptcy in 2010. During his testimony in court, Robert H. stated that he and the church had no signed agreements about book royalties, housing allowance reimbursements, or a pension plan. "We never had anything in writing. We just had an understanding, a gentleman's understanding."[16]

A Crystal Cathedral elder, Pam House, described the situation as sad and avoidable. "It didn't have to be this way. If [the Schullers] had been more open about their finances, like other churches, and worked as a team, maybe we all could have worked on this together and prevented the bankruptcy."[17]

Unfortunately, Schuller's situation is not uncommon. It can be hard to talk about money and compensation plans for retirement in the church, but the reality is, it's important. Sound organizational business practices shouldn't be avoided because it's a ministry. On the contrary, I believe the more you get your covenants and contracts in writing, the more the Lord is glorified in transition seasons.

John Maxwell recognized this need for his predecessor, Pastor Orval Butcher, at Skyline Church. John says the first thing he did at his initial board meeting at Skyline was to ask them to continue providing Pastor Butcher's salary because he had founded the church and given his entire life work to its mission and well-being. They asked how long that would be in effect. John replied, "Till he dies! And then we'll take care of his wife till she dies. And then we'll have another board meeting and decide how we can best help his kids."[18] John's focus on reverence and rightful provision for Pastor Butcher was honoring, and I honestly believe such generosity glorifies God. Now, if your church is struggling financially, this is probably a more challenging discussion to have, but it's important to find a way to honor the past service of your leaders however possible.

During the Leadership Network's simulcast on succession, William Vanderbloemen of Vanderbloemen Search Group said that it should be the responsibility of the church board to help outgoing leaders determine timelines for transition, along with helping them determine their brand and identity for life after the exchange zone. He even went so far as to suggest the board consider paying for an extensive vacation or sabbatical specifically for the outgoing leader to do some life planning. These are valuable practices to employ.

Vanderbloemen also encouraged outgoing leaders to have a coach who can speak to the board on your behalf. Sometimes someone objective can say things you simply can't say, especially when it comes to money. A coach will be able to ask the tough questions, and where possible, help secure financial compensation for the time you've invested.[19] But regardless of what the church or organization plans on your behalf, I urge you to have a solid financial plan so you can step out with confidence when the time comes.

Resistance to Change: "But no one else will do it right!"

Another stumbling block can be seen in the outgoing leader who may agree to the need for a transition, but can never fully commit to the process because he cannot accept that changes will be made under the new leadership. This leader has one foot in the door and one outside. He teeters there on the threshold between the knowledge that he needs to go and allow the church to develop, and the desire to stay and protect what he worked so hard to build.

It's important to remember that every new leader is going to have to make his or her own mistakes. An incoming leader won't do everything the way the previous leader did! It may be hard for you to accept this, but it's true regardless. Even if your successor trained under you for years, you still have to accept that he will do some things differently in order to fulfill what he believes is the vision God has given him. And he should!

I think one of the greatest gifts you can give your successor is your support and encouragement. Give him the freedom to be himself while maintaining the overarching mission of the organization. This will help you accept the changes being made more easily because you know the changes suit the new leader.

And as I said previously, never meddle, but do look for ways to be available for ongoing coaching and mentoring of your successor. You just have to make sure you can do it objectively and not critically.

My greatest advice in preparing yourself is to plan thoughtfully and pray for humility. Approach God with open hands and wait expectantly for Him to faithfully lead you. Check your motives before Him daily and ask Him to help you move away from stumbling blocks so you can get off the starting block and move ahead with excellence as you make your transition.

And as you plan and pray, hold the baton lightly. Remember, batons are meant to be carried for a time, but then they need to be passed on to the next runner. The baton isn't yours to keep, so run your leg well and pass the baton as well as you possibly can.

EVERY TEAM NEEDS A GAME PLAN

Preparing for the Win

It's better to look ahead and prepare than to look back and regret.

—JACKIE JOYNER-KERSEE[1]

E very coach will tell you that preparation is the key to victory. The legendary coach Bear Bryant of the University of Alabama exemplified this principle in the 1960s by preparing his team at least one hour for every minute they would play on the field. This means his preparation time was a minimum of sixty hours a week for a sixty-minute game. That may seem like a lot of prep time, but I believe his record speaks for itself. During his twenty-five-year tenure at Alabama, he earned six national championships and thirteen conference championships. He also held the record for most collegiate football wins at the time of his retirement, with 323. If he were still alive today, I believe he would point back to preparation as the most important factor in his team's success.

When it came time to think about our transition at Christ Fellowship, the football coach in me was convinced that the future success of such a monumental exchange in leadership would be contingent upon our preparation for it. Accordingly, I started discussing my plans to transition five years ahead of time with my family. Then, three years out, we started laying out a transition plan of how it would actually unfold. And one year out, we formalized our plan and went public with our intentions to make the exchange. And of course, the roll-out of our plan took a lot of preparation.

> WHEN YOU PREPARE FOR TRANSITION EFFECTIVELY, YOU STABILIZE YOUR ORGANIZATION AND GIVE SECURITY TO YOUR PEOPLE.

When you prepare for transition effectively, you stabilize your organization and give security to your people, which then positions you for a smooth and successful exchange. Without proper preparation, transitions can cause great turbulence for everyone.

FAILING TO PLAN IS PLANNING TO FAIL

Dr. D. James Kennedy was the founding pastor of Coral Ridge Presbyterian Church in Fort Lauderdale, Florida, and served there for forty-seven years. Dr. Kennedy was a well-known voice in culture, who advocated for the conservative values of our nation along with other great champions of the conservative movement, like Dr. James Dobson, Dr. Billy Graham, and the late Dr. Jerry Falwell. His pulpit was a platform for truth and virtue, and Coral Ridge was set on a national stage. He was a highly esteemed, dearly loved, and powerful man of God.

When Dr. Kennedy gave his sermon on Christmas Eve of 2006, no one thought it would be his last. But four days later, he suffered a cardiac arrest, which caused short-term memory loss and impaired speech. After several months of rehabilitation he was still unable to return to the pulpit. Realizing he would probably never be well enough to lead as he had previously, he retired on August 26, 2007. Sadly, Dr. Kennedy died just ten days later at the age of seventy-six.

Faced with tremendous grief, the devastated church body at Coral Ridge was left to not only cope with the loss of their beloved pastor, but also face the fact that they didn't have a plan for who would step into the pulpit once filled by such an icon of the faith.

A search committee began the frantic hunt to find a leader of a caliber similar to their predecessor. Three times they asked Dr. Billy Graham's grandson Tullian Tchividjian if he would take on the position as their new pastor, and three times Tchividjian said no. Just five years earlier he had started a church called New City Presbyterian and it was growing, so he didn't want to abandon his ministry there. Tchividjian also knew he would be following a founder of a very nationally prominent church, and that anyone thrust into that position had a good chance of failing within a few short years. And he resisted the position because he had seen that even though attendance was dropping in the latter years of Coral

Ridge's ministry, the leadership at Coral Ridge was opposed to making any changes. With all of these considerations, he didn't see how his taking the position would work.

The fourth time the committee approached him, they asked if he would consider participating in regular weekly meetings between the leadership of New City and Coral Ridge to see if they could make a merger happen. Knowing that option would afford him an opportunity to keep the church he had planted, Tchividjian agreed. For months, they met to discuss the challenges and issues that needed to be hammered out before a formal agreement could be reached. With a joint focus on unity and love, the two merged churches happily held their first service with Tchividjian as their new pastor on Easter Sunday 2009. But sadly, a few weeks of bliss and excitement were quickly replaced with division and strife.

Tchividjian and his family became the targets of many unhappy church members who felt he was too different from his predecessor, Kennedy. They believed that he didn't value their traditions and made too many changes too quickly. He had let go of some staff members for a variety of undisclosed reasons, simply stating that the personnel changes were necessary for the health of the church. He spoke less about political issues in his sermons and refused to don the traditional vestments they were accustomed to seeing on their platform, instead preferring a suit and tie. He also preferred more contemporary worship than Coral Ridge had experienced previously.

Many people had a hard time adapting to the drastic changes. Some choir members regularly got up and walked out when he started preaching. People grabbed him in the hallway after services and told him he was ruining the church, and they would do whatever they could to stop him. He left the church on one occasion to find his car had been keyed. Anonymous letters of character assassination were distributed to the church body. And a petition was circulated calling for his removal.

After six long months of pain from personal attacks and lies, the church still voted to retain Tchividjian as their senior pastor. At that time, approximately four hundred members left to start their own church, but those who remained were loyal and strong. They rallied to support Tchividjian's vision to focus on fellowship and fostering community. He worked hard to help the church ease into its new identity as a local church and not a political platform. And he created new initiatives to reach out to the community in love, for the sake of the gospel. Since then, God has done a great work among them, and they are stronger than ever.[2]

Looking back, I can't help but wonder why a church of such stature and legacy didn't already have a transition plan in place. Why hadn't Dr. Kennedy raised up a successor well before his illness? Why hadn't the board encouraged such planning? Like many churches, they didn't look forward and prepare for change.

I think Tullian Tchividjian's humility and his faithful perseverance to God's calling have upheld him as a tremendous leader at Coral Ridge. However, had there been a documented, board-supported transition plan in place, a well-prepared leader to step up before Kennedy's death, and an understanding by the congregation of how the plan would be executed, I believe they could have avoided the heartache they experienced in what turned out to be a very messy transition.

Don't let this happen to your church. Take the time to put together a game plan for transition. It will help you prepare for the future, and it will help your leadership teams and congregation pass the baton of leadership smoothly. And in the end it will create stability and security for the years ahead.

COMMUNICATING THE PLAN

In my opinion, the single most important ingredient in preparing for transition is communication. Once you have come up with a process and timetable for your transition, you must effectively communicate the transition to others in order to position your organization for long-term health, growth, and prosperity.

I can pretty much guarantee that if you fail to communicate well during a season of transition, it will make it very difficult for everyone involved. A lack of clarity and direction always causes confusion. And when people are confused, they will naturally come to their own conclusions about a situation. This can be catastrophic for you, your successor, and the organization.

If you are the senior leader of your organization, these are the steps you will need to take related to communication:

1. Talk to your family

To whom should you communicate first? I believe your first conversation needs to be with your family. They are the closest to you, and it is always best to pray and discuss such a substantial change with your home team first.

Donna and I have served in the local church every weekend since we got married. Loving God and loving people has been our mission statement for our whole life together. And our two children, Todd and Noelle, were "all in" with us as we served together through the years as a family. Naturally, transitioning was a family decision we made together.

In his book *Transition Plan*, Bob Russell talked about the adjustments a leader has to make during a time of transition, and he emphasized how important it is to consider how those adjustments would affect one's family. He admitted that this was an area he could have given more attention to during his transition at Southeast Christian. He was particularly remiss in not considering his wife's feelings about the transition. He said, "I didn't anticipate that she would have the degree of apprehension about it that she did."[3]

In my situation, I had been processing the changes in my own mind for a long time. But I hadn't given enough thought to how it might affect Donna. She had been by my side from the beginning of our ministry, always adding value wherever she could. She started and provided leadership to a number of ministries, led our women's ministry, and ministered to our pastors' wives in our home each month for many years. She was also our first choir director, and she started our prayer ministry. She was an integral part of every aspect of our ministry life together.

Christ Fellowship had been growing so rapidly that the timing to talk together thoroughly about the emotional impact of the pending transition just seemed to slip past us. Now, we all knew the transition would take place eventually, but I underestimated the importance of having more discussions and times of prayer together. We were all looking forward to and thankful for Todd's leadership, but in retrospect, I believe perhaps my focus was too narrow in how it would affect each of us differently. If I had it to do again, I would be more intentional about taking more time to talk and process the impact of the changes with my family.

> MY ADVICE TO YOU IS TO MAKE SURE YOU REMEMBER YOU ARE NOT TRANSITIONING ALONE; IT'S A FAMILY AFFAIR. CHANGE IMPACTS EVERYONE.

My advice to you is to make sure you remember you are not transitioning alone; it's a family affair. Change impacts everyone, and there needs to be time given to each family member to process and discuss the impact of those changes, so everyone is running at the same speed for a smooth transition.

2. Talk to your board

After you have talked to your family and prepared them, I believe the next conversations need to take place with the governing board at your church or organization.

At Christ Fellowship, these conversations occurred frequently and very naturally over the years because most of the members of our board of elders have been with us since the church started thirty years ago. They have provided wisdom and leadership to

Todd and me since the church's conception and were well aware of our intention to make the transition between the two of us at some point down the road.

A few years out, when I began sensing the time was approaching to make the exchange complete and formal, we began praying together as a board, specifically, for clarity about the exact timing. Then as we met for our monthly meetings we would discuss issues pertaining to Todd's readiness and the things I was doing to prepare him and the church for the exchange between us.

The elders at Christ Fellowship perceive their role as one of support and oversight. They nurture Todd and me, and provide wisdom and discernment through prayer and discussion. They are our confidants and our counsel, providing a spiritual covering and accountability. And they always have our best interests at heart. Because of that, we were very confident they would support our decision at the right time and would help us lay out the plan for making the exchange formal.

However, I recognize that you may not be in the same situation. Perhaps you are the pastor of a board-led church, where all the directional decisions are made by the board and then implemented under your leadership. If that is the case, you may rightly feel intimidated to propose a plan for transition, for fear that your job will be in jeopardy if your intentions are misunderstood. Perhaps you are wrestling with the idea of having to be so vulnerable in approaching your board to suggest a plan and timeline for transition. While I understand your hesitation, I cannot emphasize enough how important it is to devise a transition plan that will safeguard your church and mobilize your leaders to make decisions and help bring about continued growth and health after you are gone. This is a discussion that simply cannot be overlooked or underemphasized. It's that important.

As I've talked with other pastors in this position, I've encouraged them to begin the discussion by having a candid one-on-one conversation with the most influential person on their board. Doing this should help take the pressure off having to float the idea of transition with the whole group and allow you to share your heart in safety. Sharing it with the most influential person on the board will also be advantageous because that individual is often a leader in steering how your proposal will be received. If you can get that board member's buy-in and support, the transition plans will be far easier to share with everyone else.

With the wisdom and encouragement you glean from that conversation, you can then set up one-on-one meetings with the remaining board members to discuss your intentions and desires for a healthy transition. After that, you can meet collectively to hash out the details and make plans. Remember, as a leader, your job is to always be looking ahead and planning for what's around the bend, whether it's months or years down the road.

3. Talk to your key leaders and donors

After you've had the necessary conversations with your board, you will want to begin sharing your plans with other key leaders. In our transition at Christ Fellowship, I met one-on-one with the key leaders and donors who had helped implement the vision cast under my leadership over the previous twenty-seven years. I felt it was very important for them to hear the plan for my transition from me directly, before the news became general knowledge.

They had significantly invested their time, talents, and resources in the projects and programs I had implemented over the years. I wanted to make sure I honored them by acknowledging their value to me and my gratitude for their service. These one-on-one meetings gave me an opportunity to discuss the plan and allowed them to ask questions and challenge the process or the timetable. It was also important for me to make sure they understood how much it meant to me for them to support Todd in the next leg of the race for Christ Fellowship.

4. Talk to your staff

Once I'd had these conversations over the course of a few weeks, Todd and I began meeting with the executive team on our staff. These select individuals provide directional oversight to the rest of our staff and to the ministries, programs, and people of the church. When we met, we systematically laid out the purpose, plan, process, and timetable for them. Then we spent time communicating their important role in supporting and communicating the plan, so they would be prepared before we formally shared our plans at a weekly staff meeting.

Fortunately, we intended to take a few years to make our transition. And Todd was already the executive pastor, helping lead the day-to-day operations of the church for some time. As a result, the formal announcement to staff came with very little confusion or anxiety, because they were already accustomed to Todd's leadership. At that meeting, we expressed our intention to co-pastor for a year before making the exchange. In retrospect, I believe this was one of the healthiest things we did in communicating our transition to staff. It gave everyone some room for adjustment before the formal exchange, even as Todd gradually assumed leadership in many respects informally.

> ## BE SENSITIVE TO YOUR STAFF'S ABILITY TO ADAPT IN BIG LEADERSHIP TRANSITIONS.

It's important to be sensitive to your staff's ability to adapt in big leadership transitions. If you think of your church as a battleship and not a kayak, you'll recognize that you have to calculate your turns. You can't make sharp, fast turns with a huge battleship. You have to be patient and deliberate to avoid disaster.

5. Talk to your volunteers

Once the staff was aware of our intentions, we unveiled the transition plan to our ministry champions, representing about two thousand volunteers from our seven campuses. We already met with them as a group once a quarter, to encourage and celebrate their service. We also used that time to cast vision for upcoming programs or events before sharing them with the congregation at large. In this situation, it still was the right step to let them in on the news before the rest of the congregation, so we intended to share our plans at our quarterly meeting so we could honor them first and then make the announcement.

Remember that your volunteers are your core, undergirding the ministry of the church. I highly suggest that if at all possible, you let them know your transition plans early, so they can be supportive when word spreads and questions are asked. Members of that group will be the catalysts for the enthusiasm and excitement you want to have in a transition of such magnitude.

And with those who verbalize their disappointment in the transition plan or your choice for a successor, be very quick to redirect the conversation to one of praise and focus on the future. Reinforce with them that it is a spiritual decision that the Holy Spirit confirmed with the entire leadership of the church. Your goal in communicating a transition is unity; and you must do everything you can to uphold the plan with your volunteers.

6. Talk to your congregation

The weekend after the volunteer meeting, we shared our plan with the congregation. At the same time, on our website we posted a letter from our elders explaining the transition. This ensured that those who had missed the weekend service and the public would have the opportunity to find out.

After co-pastoring with Todd for a year, we dedicated a weekend service to a formal ceremony to formally exchange the baton from me to Todd. Our board of elders and John Maxwell anointed Todd and his wife, Julie. They also publicly thanked Donna and me for our years of senior leadership. I had an opportunity to reemphasize the plan for my continued role on the team, and to express my support for and excitement about the future. And Todd had an opportunity to reflect on the heritage of the past and cast vision for the future.

We celebrated the announcement that day with new titles. I moved from the position of senior pastor to founding pastor, and

Todd moved from the position of executive pastor to lead pastor. I believe this really helped the congregation have a more concrete understanding of our new roles moving forward.

Once you have a timetable for the plan and a process for disseminating that plan to others, you need to give careful consideration to *what* you will actually communicate. I think there are some important things to consider:

Communicate the things that are not changing.

When it comes to hearing that a leadership transition is going to take place, many people automatically worry about what is going to change, or what will be lost by the change. I think that's a very natural tendency, but I believe it's important for the leaders to redirect any feelings of sadness or anxiety about leadership changes, and remind people to celebrate the things that won't change. This brings a sense of security to your people, while still helping them understand the need for the change.

The first thing Todd and I wanted everyone to understand was that our core values weren't changing. We wanted to assure them that the things that had long identified the culture at Christ Fellowship would stay the same. The core values would always be central to our identity as a church family, and no one needed to fear a radical shift in priorities. Todd and I had worked together for more than twenty-five years to create the culture in which those values were embedded, and that simply was not going to change.

We also made sure everyone knew our overall mission for the church wasn't changing. Our mission statement had always been

"We are called to impact our world with the love and message of Jesus Christ." When Todd became lead pastor, he simply added the tag line "Everyone, Everyday, Everywhere" (to encourage corporate unity, commitment, and responsibility to our mission). This additional sentiment still directly reflected our core values. There was nothing new about it philosophically. We were still driven by the same mission to love people and share the truth.

However, if you rebrand your logo or your mission statement, I believe it does help highlight a new season of ministry (particularly during a leadership transition). These little changes fuel excitement and should be celebrated. They also give the successor the opportunity to put his stamp on the church.

The other big thing that wasn't going to change was our team approach to ministry, and we wanted our people to know that. Because I am an old coach, I had approached all ministry and programming from a team perspective, organizing all ministry in teams. Again, that did not change. In fact, I think it has only been enhanced. Because Todd was our executive pastor for so long, and because of the leadership tendencies in his generation, he approaches much of what he does from a collaborative perspective.

And the final thing that we communicated wouldn't change was my presence. As I mentioned previously, Todd and I work well together. We both agreed that I should stay on and help in specific areas. Even though Todd's leadership was accepted across the board, it did bring a sense of calm for some to know that he and I would still be working together, just with role changes.

Whatever the situation is in your transition, spend some time with your successor and your board of overseers managing the transition to determine what things will remain the same. Plan to communicate that information strategically. Those things will prove to be stabilizers for your people as they accompany you through a season of change.

Be clear about the team role in transition.

I would venture to say that most people's first thought when hearing about a change in leadership is, "How will this change affect me?" The prospect of change of any kind often provokes feelings of anxiety in people. The fifth-century Greek historian Herodotus said, "Diseases almost always attack men when they are exposed to a change."[4] Change can be very stressful and difficult to accept because of all the unknowns.

> ALFRED NORTH WHITEHEAD SAID OF CHANGE: "WE THINK IN GENERALITIES, BUT WE LIVE IN DETAILS."

As the one leading through transition, you need to remember what British philosopher Alfred North Whitehead said about change: "We think in generalities, but we live in details."[5] As those making the transition, we tend to think of the changes associated with transitions in a broader sense. This is because we have a bigger scope of what, why, how, and when things will take place. But our people need the specific clarity that only we can provide as leaders, because they live and thrive in the details.

Many will question how their own relationship with the outgoing leader and incoming leader will change. And some will even wonder how their response to the change will impact their future with the organization. These are very real concerns that shouldn't be overlooked or under-appreciated by the leadership.

In preparation for this book I interviewed some of our directional leaders and campus pastors for their candid feedback on how they felt the transition went. One of the questions I asked them was, "How did the transition personally affect your role/team/ministry here at Christ Fellowship?" One of our campus pastors, Jonathan Bonar, said, "I had a great personal relationship with Pastor Tom and hadn't had the life experience with Pastor Todd, so it was a little sad for me because of my relationship to him. I didn't think I'd have as much time with him, but the truth is I actually have more time with Pastor Tom now and I've grown in my relationship with Pastor Todd."[6]

It's important to give careful consideration to your team members' feelings. Keep reminding your team of how valuable they are to you and how much you love them. Try to decipher how the transition is affecting each of them individually, and then have conversations whenever necessary to clarify any areas of uncertainty. Take nothing for granted, and don't assume that just because you talked once about the details, they understand or feel any better! Most of your team will not ask the real questions that arise during transition because their emotions are conflicted. It will take time for some to understand and accept how the change will affect them. Being open to communicating as often as needed about the changes ahead will help your people feel your care for them. It will also help keep them involved and connected to the organization, to its leaders, and to the plan in place.

> ONE OF THE BIGGEST JOBS FOR BOTH THE OUTGOING LEADER AND THE SUCCESSOR IN TRANSITION IS TO STABILIZE THE TEAM MEMBERS BEFORE, DURING, AND AFTER THE TRANSITION.

I would say one of the biggest jobs for both the outgoing leader and the successor in transition is to stabilize the team members before, during, and after the transition. My friend Ed Bastian is the president of Delta Air Lines. A few years ago, the airline was faced with having to make a large number of changes in its business strategy, including cutbacks and productivity enhancements due to the financial crisis hitting the airline industry. Obviously no leader wants to have to make those decisions, but Ed and the leadership team at Delta handled it masterfully.

Rather than meeting with a select number of department representatives in the organization and then following up the decisions with a global memorandum, they strategically decided to address everyone in person. For example, they assembled the more than thirty thousand flight attendants in groups of four hundred to share about the situation. Then they gave each person an opportunity to offer suggestions and ask questions about the decisions being made. They discussed the pressing need for change but also provided the necessary hope that, working together, they could resurrect Delta into an industry powerhouse. It was a collaborative, transparent discussion, where his people felt heard. The simple gesture to communicate directly to the people made them feel respected. Communication was the conduit to understanding, acceptance, and respect. Thankfully, Delta came out of that slump and became one of the best airlines in the world,[7] which I believe is largely due to the thoughtful leadership of Ed and his team. You can never underestimate the importance of communication.

At Christ Fellowship, Todd and I tried to do the same thing that Ed had. We proactively met with entire departments to discuss the transition and how it might impact their ministries. This way, they would be able to anticipate any changes and be able to communicate the purpose and plan with their volunteers and the church family at large.

We found that taking a team approach to communicating the plan and being available to talk through the ramifications of the transition with our people provided greater buy-in to the plan, because everyone felt safe asking the hard questions. They also knew we were invested in their comfort through the process. As a result, they were able to help us have a smooth transition.

Clarify the vision and what new changes will take place.

Jay Passavant, the founding pastor of North Way Christian Community Church in Pennsylvania, said that communicating a clear plan for the future during their transition brought their congregation from uncertainty to anticipation.[8] Because of the communication, the people became more excited about what was being planned, and that helped them get focused on the new vision instead of dwelling on their trials of transition.

I think this is a really important point for your consideration. When your successor is announced, it's vital for this new leader to communicate early on the vision the Lord has given him or her for the future of the church or organization. This will help your people get excited about what the future holds and give them a sense of direction to move toward in the midst of change.

In the weeks after Todd and I announced our transition formally to the church family, he revealed from the pulpit the vision God had shown him and Julie through prayer. As a result, new excitement swept through our church family. Everyone was eager to build on the past and step out to pursue some new initiatives. This communication from Todd also helped people anticipate what would be different and when the changes would take place, so they could accept them sooner than they probably would have without any communication.

———

You cannot underestimate the importance of planning. Every team should have a game plan for when they get on the field to play! Take the time to think through all the aspects of transition and plan prayerfully with the team around you. And when it comes to preparing everyone for transition, you must take time to communicate well. You may feel that you have everything mapped out in your mind, but that means very little if you cannot help others see it for themselves. We can never assume that others have the same sense of direction and understanding that those involved in formulating the plan have.

Leave nothing to chance. Be very intentional about crafting your transition plan clearly and consistently before you communicate it; and then, once you have everything in place, say it again and again. And again. You cannot overcommunicate the plan! Use a number of different methods to make sure you are reaching everyone you can by every means possible. This will reduce any issues, uncertainties, or questions. I believe that as you do this, you will lay the path for a seamless transition because a game plan brings clarity, which provides security and stability.

EVERY RACE NEEDS
THE RIGHT ANCHOR

Selecting and Preparing Your Successor

It takes a leader with vision to see the future leader within the person.

—JOHN C. MAXWELL[1]

It's not lost on me that having a son who served alongside me for more than twenty-five years, and felt a calling to be my successor, is uncharacteristic of most pastors' situations. In fact, there are very few churches in which that arrangement has worked for father-son duos, even when the intention was to make the transition from father to son.

Reverend Charles Stanley spent years grooming his son Andy to one day be his successor at First Baptist Church in Atlanta, Georgia, where he had been serving as senior pastor since 1971. When Andy was in college, he abandoned plans to become a journalist in order to go into ministry at his father's church as their youth pastor. In the years following, Andy began preaching from the pulpit frequently. His talent, charisma, and wisdom were evident, so in 1992 Charles appointed Andy as the pastor over their first satellite campus. The dream of a long-term partnership that would eventually be followed by Andy's succession was being realized.

Sadly, a few years later, Charles's wife, Anna, filed for divorce. That situation, coupled with the fact that Andy's satellite was outgrowing the main campus and the differences in his leadership style and preferences were becoming obvious, led Andy to the realization that he simply could not continue on the path toward one day replacing his father at First Baptist. Carrying the weight of this reality, he entered his father's office and resigned in 1995.[2]

The dream had ended and left in its wake heartache and disappointment for both of them. Their relationship suffered as a result, but in time and with intentional conversations focused on love and healing, they have reconciled and are stronger for it. And both men now lead tremendous ministries that are having incredible kingdom impact in Atlanta and around the world.

After reading their story a while back, I got to thinking about what I would have done if I hadn't been blessed with a son who felt called to be my successor. As I said before, the reality is that very few senior leaders in the church have that benefit. Knowing my situation was a unique blessing made me contemplate what kind of leader I would have looked for in a successor if I hadn't had my son by my side, ready and able to take up the baton and run.

It would seem as though the process of selecting the right person should be as natural for senior leaders as it is for us to lead, right? I mean, we know firsthand what it takes to lead in our role. Unfortunately, many successful leaders I've spoken with have admitted that they struggled to identify the key traits and qualities necessary for another person to adequately fill their role.

If you don't yet know what your successor should look like, I would suggest you first create an introspective inventory of your skill set and leadership abilities. Then, prepare a thorough list of the position's responsibilities. This process should help you gain some clarity about the kind of leader you and your board are looking for to succeed you.

In addition to understanding which of your strengths have benefitted the organization under your leadership, it is also necessary to determine what other strengths may be needed to take the organization to the next level. One good exercise that will help you determine these leadership traits is to sit down with your team and your board to discuss your strengths and weaknesses, in light of where everyone feels the organization is headed in the future. It always helps to have a 360-degree look at your leadership—from people positioned at every angle. This is because we often do things intuitively that we might not initially identify in our own inventory. Those closest to you will be able to describe those qualities and practices so you have a well-rounded list.

Another good means of attaining key qualities to include is through discussions with leaders of churches or organizations that are at the next level up from you. This will help you learn what skills they believe are essential to be successful in leadership at that level. Analyzing their input, and applying the qualities that work in your environment to the profile of the person you're looking for, will help you be even more successful in your recruitment process.

In addition to a solid list of traits and responsibilities, you need to make sure you or your human resources department administers a battery of comprehensive emotional, spiritual, and personality tests to help you understand the makeup and maturity of the person you are considering for the position. Every person hired at Christ Fellowship takes these kinds of tests because it allows us to look for any red flags *before* we invite that individual to serve as a leader in ministry. I truly believe you can't afford to overlook any opportunity to really get to know your candidates inside and out.

NONNEGOTIABLE CHARACTERISTICS OF A SUCCESSOR

Every coach has certain criteria used to select quality team members. In professional football, the path to being drafted starts at the annual scouting combine, where potential prospects compete in a number of skills that test their athletic ability and demonstrate their strengths. If a player has the qualities a scout is looking for to fill a position on his team for the next season, he is then invited to try out for the team.

Obviously, every organization's needs are going to be different when it comes to identifying the distinctive traits and qualities the successor must possess to do his or her job well and benefit the greater good of the team. Hopefully by now you have a running list of traits and responsibilities for your successor in mind, but I want to share a universal list of characteristics that I believe to be nonnegotiable when it comes to selecting a senior leader in the church. Good church leaders do the following:

1. They Possess Character and Integrity

Character and integrity are the indispensable moral and ethical qualities of a leader. They establish what the candidate values and what he or she will or will not stand for in both public and private arenas. You must select someone of high character and moral integrity to succeed you because leadership operates on the basis of trust. People do not follow titles; they follow character, because character earns trust.

Character and integrity also reflect how well leaders lead themselves, which obviously will have a direct correlation on how they will lead those entrusted to their care. One of the ways you can see if your candidate has character and integrity is by assessing how he or she handles responsibility. Take a look at what the candidate has managed in the past—programs and people. Has he or she managed the care of both well?

> MY GRANDFATHER ALWAYS TOLD ME THAT CHARACTER IS REFLECTED IN HOW CONSCIENTIOUS WE ARE IN HANDLING THE SMALL TASKS AS WELL AS THE LARGE ONES.

My grandfather always told me that character is reflected in how conscientious we are in handling the small tasks as well as the large ones. If we take care of the small things with excellence, we will never have to worry about big things because we will handle them in the same way. Mother Teresa summarized

Jesus' admonition to be trustworthy in small things so we may be entrusted with much (Luke 16:10) by saying, "Be faithful in small things, because it is in them that your strength lies."[3] You need someone who is responsible with whatever has been asked of him or her and who operates in excellence, because excellence honors God and inspires others.

You've heard it said that a leader must guard both his public and his private life. Well, I don't believe that we can differentiate our behavior in private and in public. As leaders we are not entitled to a *private* life. I have one life, and I need to conduct myself the same, according to the values and virtues of God's Word, regardless of whether I am at home with my family or in the pulpit, preaching. Environment does not dictate my character; God does. You need to select a successor who demonstrates consistency in his or her character.

You also need a leader who honors his or her commitments. Commitment is a strong indicator of character because when we honor our word, we gain the trust of others. When leaders fail to do what they say they will do, they are seen as fickle and unreliable. You don't want a senior leader running your church who can't be trusted to show up where he needs to be or do what he needs to do to support his team and his congregation. People simply won't follow someone who isn't committed.

One clear way you can gauge your candidate's character is by interviewing his or her family. Years ago we realized how important it was to not only interview the candidate himself, but to invite his spouse to an interview as well. It's possible to learn so much more from the people who live with the candidate day in and day out. During the interview, ask a lot of interactive questions so you can observe how the two of them interact with each other. Your candidate's strengths and weaknesses will often be revealed in the context of his most important relationship. I'm convinced that if he doesn't have a strong home with harmony and balance, he will never be the effective leader you need him to be for your church family.

Because of Todd's many years of serving alongside me, everyone knew him well and could see a consistent demonstration of character in the way he lived his life and led the church. Todd always put people first and built a really strong team as our executive pastor, but he had the right boundaries in place so he could properly pour into his family, giving them the love and attention they needed. Because of that, God blessed and prospered everything he put his hand to, and he was able to establish a solid trust with our staff and congregation. This made our transition all the easier.

Since my transition, I regularly have conversations with senior leaders about whether or not they have a particular person in mind to replace them. One friend I asked said that one particular member of his staff was incredibly loyal to him and seemed to have the right skill mix needed to be the senior leader in his place, but there was one major problem inhibiting his choice. The person had eroded trust with some other staff members, and now they didn't trust him. I told him that it was obvious to me that if the team didn't trust him, he was not their man. If the staff member couldn't repair that breach of trust, he was not in a position to lead the team or the congregation. People simply won't follow someone they can't trust to lead them honestly.

If after interviewing the candidate extensively, you and your board don't feel that he has proven his character, it is absolutely essential that you take seriously the character references on his application. Take time to thoroughly interview those references. Dig into the candidate's past by interviewing people who have worked closely with him at the various levels of his leadership development. Keep in mind, however, that many people will be hesitant to say anything negative about your candidate. You may have to read between the lines, considering the reasons for vagueness and pauses. If you feel that you are not getting a full picture of his character and integrity, I would suggest you bring the potential successor onto your staff and let him prove himself among you.

2. They Are Gifted and Skilled

Psalm 78:72 says that David "shepherded [the people] with integrity of heart; with skillful hands he led them" (NIV). Integrity and skill go hand in hand. You can't have one without the other in a senior leadership position. A worthy candidate must be gifted and skilled to manage the role he is being hired to undertake. So he must be good at what he does, but even more, he must have the skills necessary to build upon the existing strengths of the organization. Without a God-given giftedness in the area he is chosen to lead and the accompanying skills necessary to get the job done, he will fail.

While it's true that not every incoming leader will have the exact same strengths as the outgoing leader, one particular skill he or she must have is the ability to effectively communicate the organization's vision and then mobilize people into action. John

Maxwell said, "If it is true that almost everything we become and accomplish in life is with and through other people, then the ability to connect and create rapport with them is the most important skill we can learn."[4] Isn't that the truth? Communication is a vital skill for all leaders. In fact, I would say many people judge a pastor's leadership ability by his communication skills, because it is the first, and sometimes the only, skill they will witness.

You also need to look for a leader who is able to engage people in their passion for the things of God and demonstrate his care for others. Connection with a spiritual leader begins when the people feel confident in the leader's devotion to God and when they feel personally valued. I have always heard it said that people don't care how much you know until they know how much you care. And they will know how much that leader cares for them by the way he communicates with them.

When I'm considering a prospective leader to join our team, I always evaluate how well he communicates in both small and large group settings. Some candidates will naturally be more relaxed because they have more experience or a more intuitive sense of effective communication. But in some cases there will be an obvious lack of natural inclination or experience from which to build. If that is the case, particularly when selecting a senior leader, you will have to accept that the candidate just doesn't have the skill set needed to lead at this level. Ralph G. Nichols said, "The number one criteria for banishment and promotion for professionals is an ability to communicate effectively."[5] I agree with him, especially when it comes to senior leadership in the church. Communication is certainly a skill that can be learned and developed with practice, but at this level the skill must already be established with excellence; otherwise, the candidate is not qualified to lead your organization.

3. They Practice Organizational Management

Leaders need to have the capacity to embrace complex environments. Accordingly, I believe that all senior leaders in the church must have organizational management skills. I understand that the larger the church, the more necessary this aspect of responsibility will be. But regardless of church size, I still believe that all senior leaders of churches today must have a comprehensive understanding of how to run the church from both a spiritual and a business perspective.

> LEADERS NEED TO HAVE THE CAPACITY TO EMBRACE COMPLEX ENVIRONMENTS.

Today's senior pastor's responsibilities entail far more than just weekly sermon preparation, visiting shut-ins, and conducting funerals and weddings. The senior pastor also must serve as president and CEO of the organization as a whole, providing oversight and leadership to budgets, building projects, diverse staff teams, and more.

There are multiple layers of processing and leading at this level that can't be overlooked or minimized when selecting your successor. Any potential pastor needs to have the education and experience to support the complexities of such responsibility. And while all pastors can and should hire a team around them that is brighter, faster, and sharper in these areas, it is still ultimately the responsibility of the senior leader to lead those teams.

4. They Are Team Builders

A leader in the church today has to be someone who can build a team. He or she must have emotional equity with your people in order to lead a growing organization. A good senior leader will be able to navigate change well, and will also be able to help everyone feel heard and empowered, so they can lead from their strengths and their place at the table. In fact, I think it is impossible to be a good leader if you aren't good at building relationships with your team members. I suggest that you look for an encouraging person who, upon walking into the room, has good rapport with the people on your team, because you want someone whom your team enjoys being with and whom they are willing to follow on the next leg of the journey.

I always look for a lifter of others when I choose leaders at any level, but this is especially vital in your successor, because the senior leader sets the tone for everyone else to follow. I want someone who will look for the good in people and help them see who God has created them to be for His glory. Your successor must be someone who can build and empower his or her team for victory.

A team builder is also a servant leader. Look for someone who is humble and will take up the figurative towel and basin for the team. A good leader should be willing to meet the needs of the people so they can be successful in reaching team goals and having kingdom impact. This person also needs to be secure and not afraid to hand off point leadership to the team.

A good indicator that your candidate is a team builder is to look at the team he most recently led. How long did his team members stay with him? If there was a lot of turnover, it might indicate that he wasn't a good team builder. If, on the other hand, he had team members who stayed with him for a long time, through many seasons of ministry, it speaks volumes about his ability to really connect, value, and empower others because a great team builder fosters loyalty in his people.

At Christ Fellowship, we have several team members who left for a period of time to serve elsewhere, and have since returned. Recently, one person who rejoined our team said, "It was a great place I went to, but no one loved me like I was loved at Christ Fellowship." Great team builders have team members who feel loved and appreciated and encouraged to fulfill their calling in ministry. I believe your senior leader should have a track record of retention, enthusiasm, and loyalty from the team he or she is leaving to lead yours.

5. They Are Fruit-Bearing

Past performance is always the greatest indicator of future performance. The individual you choose to be your successor needs to be a proven leader who has impacted others for the kingdom in the past. I truly believe that no matter the size of the church he came from, or the title or position he had previously, there should be evidence of fruit.

> PAST PERFORMANCE IS ALWAYS
> THE GREATEST INDICATOR OF
> FUTURE PERFORMANCE.

I had the chance to interview football coach Larry Coker after his 2001 University of Miami team won the national championship. When I asked him what he believed were the keys to victory for a coach, he said that no matter what level you coach, whether for a junior high or high school team, or a college or professional team, a good coach will "bloom where he's planted."[6] Leaders grow and produce fruit wherever they are called.

I remember when Donna and I were living in Georgetown, Kentucky, while I was the football coach at Georgetown College. On the weekends I served as an interim pastor at various churches in central Kentucky, while they were searching for permanent leaders. One particular church in Paris, Kentucky, was on the verge of going through a church split after their pastor left. Donna and I did our best to help them look for ways to find unity. We encouraged them and cast vision for what they could do together in that region for the kingdom of God. Not only did they stay together, but they also quadrupled in size during my time as interim pastor. They also started a bus ministry, which helped expand their children's ministry. We even cast a vision for them to buy a larger piece of property to build on for the future. And, we were able to help them look for and select their full-time pastor.

When Donna and I look back on that time of ministry, we

consider ourselves so blessed to have had a part in helping to re-vitalize that church for God's glory. Had we not invested where God called us to serve, we would have missed out on the oppor-tunity to have impact on that church and learn the leadership lessons God wanted us to learn in the early days of our ministry.

A good leader is always looking for how he can best advance the people and the mission where he has been called to lead. And truly great leaders are transformational leaders. Because of their investment and leadership, there will always be evidence of posi-tive change. People will be able to see God's hand and blessing on and through their lives.

During the interview process, I would suggest you ask your candidates to describe their greatest achievements and strengths. They need to have a track record, because it gives you something to go on, particularly if you are bringing in someone from the out-side. You need to be able to see areas of their leadership that have been successful. I truly believe that a good leader, no matter the environment, will prosper. Wherever great leaders serve, that area will demonstrate growth. They will add value to the organization, even if the situation around them is less than ideal. Simply put, a leader has a winning record.

6. They Are DNA Carriers

The personality and leadership style of your successor can (and very well may) be different from yours. Even his leadership strengths can be somewhat different, because he will build a team around him to accent his strengths and shore up his weaknesses. But one thing that cannot be different is how he fits into the church's culture. Your successor needs to appropriately live out the core values of your organization. One way to say this is that he must be a DNA carrier.

DNA is a molecule in the body that carries all the genetic and biological information about that person. I consider an organizational DNA carrier to be someone who can translate and transfer all the identifying markers of what you value to others. Just as a cell must replicate its DNA when it divides and grows, you need DNA carriers who are able to pass along your church culture's "genetics"—or values. DNA carriers understand your culture and live out the values you esteem, making sure that what gets taught and practiced is the same at all levels of your organization. We all leave genetic fingerprints on everything we touch. You can have confidence that a DNA carrier understands your identity and can pass on the markers set for them.

If you don't pass the baton to a DNA carrier, I guarantee that one of two things will happen: either the transition won't stick and the organization will be left scrambling to find a new leader, or the face of the organization will change dramatically. When you put into leadership someone whose characteristics and priorities are too different from those of the church culture, over time the DNA may morph or get distorted.

It's easy to be certain of a DNA carrier when your successor is an existing team member. He will have been around long enough to prove he understands and lives out your values. It will obviously be more challenging to identify the DNA of an outsider coming in, but if you can clearly describe your core values and how and where they are expressed within the organization, your candidate should demonstrate the potential to adopt and adapt to them. Then, once the leader is chosen, you can work more strategically to express your church's DNA and watch to see that he does adopt it. That's why this chapter includes the practices for both selection *and* preparation. There is always a learning curve; you can help the incoming leader learn and adjust where needed.

———

I believe the characteristics I have listed will provide a helpful starting place for you as you prayerfully and thoughtfully consider what kind of person will be your successor. Don't make any compromises if these characteristics are lacking in your candidates, because they are the nonnegotiables! (See 1 Tim. 3; Titus 2.)

I'll admit to making some poor hiring choices in the past. I can think of a few instances in which I focused too much on a single trait instead of considering the person as a whole. When I look back at those poor decisions, I realize I made an emotional choice based on chemistry in the interview, or because a mutual friend made the recommendation. I always tend to expect the best of people. Because of that, I've often looked at a guy who might not be a perfect match and thought I could coach him up in the areas in which he lacked. Or I believed that with a little experience in that area, he would come around. But the truth is, I overestimated my ability to compensate for his weaker traits. Instead, I should have given greater consideration to how those weaker traits would affect his ability to lead on our team, in our environment.

Don't overlook glaring weaknesses; they will manifest themselves in time, causing a lot of grief and strife for everyone. And as you can imagine, this is even more important when you are hiring the person who will lead your entire organization! Invest heavily on the front end of your hiring process. Don't leave any questions unasked; do your research, and pray. Insist on these qualities and this caliber of leadership, and I believe God can fill in the rest of what's needed.

RECRUITING A SUCCESSOR

Once you know what you are looking for in a successor, you have to go about the arduous task of finding one. In some situations, finding your successor will be pretty easy because he or she has served as your right hand for a number of years. Or maybe the person you are considering is already a leader in another area of your organization and you see potential to raise him up for a new role.

There are a lot of benefits to selecting someone who already serves with you. You will likely know him intimately and be able to easily see how his gifts and strengths match up with the needs of the position. Plus, you will be able to head off any difficulties he might have in your role because you are well acquainted with his weaknesses as well. Also, as I mentioned earlier, he will already be a DNA carrier. He will probably have a lot of loyalty to the culture and mission of your organization, which will provide a lot of security for the team and those you lead. All of these reasons make a very compelling argument for hiring inside your organization.

One church doing this well is Gateway Church in Southlake, Texas. I recently spoke with Todd Lane, one of their executive senior pastors. His dad, Tom, is the lead executive senior pastor. The Gateway team is currently working on a transition plan for multiple levels of senior leadership years in advance of the actual transitions so they are well prepared when the time comes to make those exchanges.

It has benefitted them greatly to start conversations early because it allows them to be proactive in helping their outgoing leaders with an exit strategy that works for them while enabling them to have intentional mentoring conversations with leaders being identified for those senior-level positions. Todd said, "Upcoming leaders are being invited into conversations about the transition, and with enough advanced notice the transitions begin to happen in a methodical way. This will allow the upcoming leader to glean from the outgoing leader and essentially be able to learn on the job while the outgoing leader is still present to mentor them through it."[7] It's clear that when these identified leaders are already DNA carriers on your team, you have a great opportunity to integrate them into a shared role much sooner, easing much of the discomfort and growing pains that come with leadership transitions.

Of course, in some situations, you may not feel confident that your next leader is among your current team members. Perhaps no one on your team has sensed a calling from the Lord to step up into the lead role. Maybe no one's strengths or personality matches up with what is needed to take the organization to the next level. Sometimes an organization simply needs a fresh face to help rebuild or recharge the energy and momentum. These situations warrant bringing in an outsider. You may even need to employ an executive search firm to help you find some potential candidates who will match up well with your unique identity and needs as an organization.

As far as having eligible family members is concerned, I will caution you that senior leadership in the church shouldn't be viewed as something to be inherited! It has to be a clear calling from God. For us at Christ Fellowship, it was apparent to our congregation and leadership that Todd had not only the anointing and leadership ability, but also the church's DNA. This made him the obvious choice to succeed me. Though we didn't frequently discuss it, there was really no doubt in anyone's mind that he would eventually take over.

After recognizing Todd's role as our leader in the next leg of the race for God's ministry through Christ Fellowship, my role was to prepare him and make sure we were executing the transition at the right time. Then we could make sure we seized and sustained the momentum of our church ministry. Todd was more than ready when the time came, and he has done a tremendous job. He was the perfect choice, and God is using him mightily in ways none of us could have anticipated.

In contrast, some of my friends who have sons realized that their sons either had other gifts or didn't sense a calling from God to take up their mantle of leadership. This caused great disappointment for some of them, because it left them with no one in the wings ready to take up where they left off. But at the same time, my friends considered themselves fathers first. This meant

they simply encouraged their sons to do whatever God was calling them to do, even if it wasn't in ministry. Other friends had no
family member at all to consider.

If you find yourself in one of those scenarios, the best thing
you can start doing today is raising up leaders within your organization. Your effort may position them to be uniquely qualified
to take up positions of leadership after you are gone. That's why I
spent time in chapter 3 emphasizing the importance of empower-
ing your team. It is so important that we raise up leaders around
us. They will become the extensions of our ministry and the face
of the future leadership team.

The apostle Paul gave us a great example of being a spiritual
father in his own ministry. He knew he couldn't fulfill his calling
to establish the church if he stayed in only one location, but he
also wisely recognized the need to have someone there to oversee
and disciple the people in those churches, so he chose leaders and
trained them to help share the load. In all, he raised up eighteen
spiritual sons to pastor and lead the churches he planted in the
first century.

My friend Larry Stockstill has done an outstanding job of raising up not only his biological sons in ministry, but also twenty-eight
spiritual sons who are now leading some of the greatest churches
in America and across the globe. In his book *The Surge*, he wisely
said, "Partners will determine your accomplishments, but spiritual sons will determine your legacy. Partners operate while you
are alive, but sons continue after you are gone."[8]

What a fantastic reminder! Ministry partners definitely get
things done. Hand in hand we fulfill the vision. But the training,

loyalty, common thinking, and passion for your ministry of a son (natural or spiritual) will carry your work into the next generation with him. Regardless of whether or not you have a biological son ready to take the baton, you need to be intentional about raising up spiritual sons. On a football team, the bench represents the additional players who are ready and capable of entering the game when needed. The "deeper" your bench, the longer your list of potential successors and the wider your organization's reach.

And don't wait till it's too late! Start today the process of selecting your successor by determining the characteristics of the ideal candidate. Then find some men who match up and begin investing in their lives so they can begin to have impact on the next generation. This is so important for your organization. I can assure you that the time you spend identifying potential successors will not be wasted, because it will benefit the organization in the long term.

PREPARING YOUR SUCCESSOR

If it is partially or wholly your responsibility to select your successor, it will probably also be your responsibility to prepare that new leader for the exchange. I would highly suggest that you build in plenty of time for preparation before the transition, because it will take some time to get your successor ready to take over your position. This is not something that can be rushed, if you want the transition to go smoothly. In fact, I would say you need a minimum of one to three years to really prepare your successor and to establish your team's confidence in his or her ability and leadership.

Sometimes, because of the nature of your transition or the structure of your organization, you may not be able to actively participate in your successor's preparation. I'm primarily speaking to the leader who has the flexibility to help select and prepare the person who will replace him or her. Still, if you are not in a position to make that decision, it will be advantageous for you to do everything you possibly can to smooth your successor's transition. Following are a few ways I suggest you go about preparing your successor for his or her new role:

1. Develop your successor's communication skills

In our case at Christ Fellowship, Todd had been leading as the executive pastor for many years. He was more than prepared to run the day-to-day operations of the church and provide oversight to the staff and our various ministry teams. What he needed most during our time of preparation was more pulpit time. Todd was a good communicator, but he only preached when I was traveling or otherwise indisposed. Because of that, many in our congregation didn't know Todd as well as they knew me.

So a few years before our transition officially took place, we created a teaching schedule that would expose the people to Todd on a more regular basis and help him gain more experience in overseeing the weekend worship experience. Initially Todd took on 30 percent of the preaching in a calendar year. Later we bumped him up to 50 percent, where he stayed for a couple of years. By the time we had passed the baton, he was teaching 60 percent of the time. Then, in the first year he served as lead pastor, he spoke 70 percent of the time. This left the other 30 percent to be shared between me, John Maxwell, and guest speakers.

This gradual progression allowed Todd to take on more responsibility to be the lead pastor. It also helped slowly acclimate our congregation to the plan for him to take over in time.

I have a friend in our congregation whom I'll call "Uncle Larry." He came to me during the preparation phase for the transition and said, "Well, I have no doubt that Todd will do great with the administrative leadership of the church, but he will never be able to live up to your standard of teaching on the weekends." My response to Uncle Larry was, "Give him some time, and you will see him grow to become a great communicator of the Word." A year after the transition, Uncle Larry came up to me and said, "You were right. Todd has become a great communicator. I think he is even better than his dad." As I'm sure you can imagine, there is no sweeter music to a father's ear than when others see in his child what he sees.

The point is that you have to help hone your successor's communication skills. If you don't already have a regular schedule that allows your successor to preach, you need to formulate a plan to do so. Once you are confident that he will succeed you, it is so important that you give him pulpit time to gain credibility and experience. Perhaps you will want to start by inviting him to co-preach with you periodically. Then you need to schedule him into your preaching calendar and build up his pulpit time. As you near the handoff, he needs to eventually preach more than you do. Two good resources for developing a person's communications skills are John Maxwell's book *Everyone Communicates, Few Connect* and Ken Davis's book *Secrets of Dynamic Communication.*

2. Allow your successor to show leadership at special services or events

When Dave Stone was transitioning into his role as successor to Bob Russell, in addition to increasing his pulpit time, Bob gave him the opportunity to speak on special occasions and even peak times, like Easter and Christmas. As Dave looked back at his preparation, he felt this was one of the most impactful things Bob did to prepare him, because it helped the people view him as an equal to Bob in leadership, which in turn helped them accept him sooner.

Recently I was checking out Southeast Christian Church's website and noticed that Kyle Idleman, the pastor slated to succeed Dave, had given the sermon at their Christmas Eve services this year. Clearly Dave has remembered how Bob prepared him with some prime weekend speaking slots, and is doing the same for Kyle.

What I love is that there was no pride on Bob's part. He sincerely wanted the best for Dave and the organization. He didn't cling to those big events or special services with a sense of entitlement, because he knew that it was in Dave's best interest to be given those opportunities. He stood back and cheered in public, and then coached in private.

That's your responsibility as an outgoing leader. Giving those important spots to your successor highlights the value you place on him, which elevates his influence with others. As Todd took on more pulpit time, I sat on the front row, cheering for him and affirming him before the congregation. I wanted people to see that I believed in him and would honor him as our new leader. There is no substitute for your public enthusiasm and influence. When you publicly affirm your successor, you send a message to your congregation about how much you trust and believe in him. What events or services do you need to give up to help your successor get the experience and credibility he needs to take over when you're gone?

3. Let your successor take over leadership of staff and board meetings

In addition to the increased pulpit time, I asked Todd to lead the elder and staff meetings. I knew that even though Todd had been overseeing our ministry teams, as senior leader I was still viewed as the ultimate decision maker. It was important that our teams start shifting to view Todd as their leader. By leading the meetings, he was able to assert his leadership and inject his own personality. Not only did he gain confidence and experience, but he also gained influence with our leadership. In the same way, you need to come up with a plan for gradually integrating your successor's voice and influence into leadership meetings.

First, meet with your successor before leadership meetings to talk through your agenda and coach him on how to approach the issues at hand. It is particularly helpful to start by giving him ownership of winning ideas. If you have a good idea for future programming or something of that nature, share it with your successor and encourage him to make the proposal. Then you can do everything in your power to affirm his suggestion in the meeting and praise him publicly. In the meantime, you can still tackle the sticky situations or difficult conversations until he has a few wins under his belt. Then you will be ready to coach him on how to navigate the more challenging conversations.

4. Encourage your successor to manage the finances and develop relationships with key donors

When I was grooming Todd to take over, I challenged him to develop closer relationships with some of our major donors—people who had sacrificed to make the mission and purpose of Christ Fellowship a reality. This was an area he had not been part of as our executive pastor. I'm sure he would be the first to admit that it was not the most comfortable addition to his responsibilities. At the same time, he knew that those relationships were important, so the time and energy needed to step out of his comfort zone was beneficial.

Frankly, it's my conviction that anyone leading a church needs to have some background in management and good business sense. A good leader has to understand how to construct and manage a budget, how to raise funds for building campaigns or special projects, how to teach his church family to be faithful tithers and generous givers, and how to build trust and equity with potential and existing donors. For the church to thrive in the future, there is no way around this aspect of your successor's training and preparation. You need to make sure he is well acquainted with the ins and outs of the church finances. To do so, you will need to talk through with him how decisions were made in the past and why certain allocations are more important than others. You will also want to take him along to meetings with donors and involve him in any immediate financial decisions that will impact the future of the church and his oversight as the new leader.

5. Introduce your successor to other leaders of influence

I encouraged Todd to start building relationships with other ministry leaders outside our church's four walls, because it's important to partner with other strong, godly organizations to fulfill the Great Commission. I started taking Todd with me when I was invited to speak at conferences or meet with new leaders of influence. This way, he could interact with them and lay the foundation for partnerships that could be formed for the future health and impact of Christ Fellowship.

For example, Christ Fellowship had financially supported EQUIP, the nonprofit John Maxwell formed to train Christian leaders around the world. I had served on their board for a number of years, but Todd wasn't actively involved in serving with them because of his responsibilities at the church and his pursuit of his master's and doctorate degrees. When I knew he had more margin to begin building new relationships and take on new initiatives, I introduced him to some of the key leaders at EQUIP, and he built relationships with their team. One result of building those new relationships was that Todd traveled to Europe as a trainer for them, to develop ministry leaders there.

Think about the relationships that have catapulted your ministry or your own leadership to new levels. What partnerships have you made that could potentially have great impact on the future of the organization under your successor's leadership? Who do you need to introduce your successor to as you prepare him to take over the leadership of your church?

6. Put your successor in the center of your world

As we approached the transition, I pulled Todd into the center of the world that soon would become his. Don't neglect this important practice as an outgoing leader. Take an inventory of the things your successor would never otherwise be exposed to, and think about what you wish someone had done to prepare you. What areas do you wish you had been better prepared to lead? What existing programs and relationships require a deeper context that only you can provide to your successor? Once you have your list, discuss those things with your successor and come up with a game plan for making sure you adequately prepare him in each area. Remember, your succession plan is not a success if your successor fails because you failed to prepare him!

––––––

If you are familiar with the intricacies of team relays in the sport of track and field, then you know the anchor runner is ultimately responsible for getting the baton across the finish line. This final runner in the relay must have a great kick and a strong desire to win that will drive him, whether he's running from behind or from the lead. The anchor runner must be a strong leader, able to carry the team, no matter the circumstances when the baton is passed to him.

Likewise, every church needs to select the best possible person to succeed their current leader. In fact, the transition plan crafted by you and your board will only be as good as the selection and preparation of the person chosen to succeed you. Great teams don't happen by accident. They are created with intent and by design.

> ## GREAT TEAMS DON'T HAPPEN BY ACCIDENT.

As my friend John Maxwell put it, "Everything rises and falls on leadership."[9] It's important to keep that admonition at the forefront of your mind during this process, because the individual you and/or the board choose will determine whether or not your organization will thrive after you leave. You only get one shot at getting this right, so you had better be very thorough in developing and implementing a process for the selection and preparation of your successor.

 5

TIPS FOR ANCHOR RUNNERS: POSITIONING YOURSELF FOR SUCCESS

If I have seen farther than others, it is because I
was standing on the shoulders of giants.

—ISAAC NEWTON

'll never forget when Todd walked in to lead a staff meeting for
the first time after we had announced the transition from my
leadership to his. I felt a little surge of anxious energy from him as
we entered the room filled with a couple hundred staff members,
key volunteers, and interns. As they waited for him to step up
and shepherd them as their new leader, he leaned over to me and
said, "Wow, Dad. I had no idea how much responsibility you carried in so many areas." Of course, he knew many of the burdens
that came with senior leadership, but I think it became more official for him that day when he felt the gravity of being the number
one guy. I responded as any dad would: I laughed and told him I
loved him. Then I pushed him toward the stage and went to find
my seat.

If you're the leader who has been chosen to receive the baton, even if you prepare well before you take on your new role, there are some things you simply can't know until you are actually in your position, functioning as the new leader. But I can offer some great tips to you, based on the lessons Todd and I learned during our baton exchange at Christ Fellowship.

NINE THINGS YOU MUST DO TO RECEIVE THE BATON WELL

1. Be patient

For many years, Todd and I both knew the day would come when I would turn over the leadership of the church to him, but the exact time was mine to determine. I talk to a lot of guys who know they are next in line to lead, and they are chomping at the bit to take over. If you are feeling that way, be patient. I remember one day when Todd and I were talking about our transition in my office and he said, "Dad, the baton is yours to give, not mine to take."

> "DAD, THE BATON IS YOURS TO GIVE, NOT MINE TO TAKE."

Our transition would not have gone nearly as well as it did if Todd had pushed me on the timing. As the senior pastor, it was my job to determine the best timing for Todd, our church, and our team so we could be sure to execute a smooth pass of the baton. In the meantime, Todd's job was to continue to prepare himself for that day and to be faithful to the current tasks he was responsible for, knowing his time to lead would come when it was best.

Communication between you and your predecessor will help you have a clear understanding of his intentions, but in the meantime, your goal is to be patient and faithful to your calling today. Prepare as much as possible for the future role you will be given, but be dependable and supportive wherever God has you now. God will never waste your time! He has you right where He wants you. Trust Him to provide peace and wisdom regarding the timing for you to take the lead.

2. Be yourself

One of the more challenging obstacles you will face as a successor is the pressure to be like your predecessor. It can be really hard to follow someone who was greatly loved and admired. I mean, let's face it; few are enthusiastic about losing a strong leader. If your predecessor is leaving on good terms and making a transition when his leadership is still vibrant and the organization is healthy, no one will want to see him go.

In my case, I would like to believe that no one *wanted* me to step down. I was still young and had a lot of energy and excitement about the ministry God was orchestrating at Christ Fellowship. In fact, I could easily say that at the time I handed off the baton we were actually enjoying one of the most prosperous seasons in the history of the church. But because of that, I knew the timing was right for Todd to take the lead. We both had peace that it was

God's will and timing, and this helped me step down and him to step up to his calling. But that doesn't mean it made sense to everyone in our congregation.

While Todd and I have some similar leadership traits, we are also very different. In the run-up to the transition, I made sure I encouraged him in his strengths, so he wouldn't worry about how our differences might be received by our church family. I knew Todd simply had to be himself and lean in to the ways he believed God was leading him, even as he stood firm on the foundation of our past. The commonality between us lies in our commitment to the mission and core values of the church. None of that changed as a result of our transition, which brought a lot of peace and stability during our exchange.

Along with our similarities, Todd needed to assess the values he brought as a leader and leverage those things in the decisions he made and through the interactions he had with those he led. It took a conscious effort to try not to be me or anyone else, but to just be himself and find confidence in who he was and what God was calling him to do.

My friend Joel Osteen had to overcome a great deal of pressure to be like his father when he took over as pastor of Lakewood Church in Texas. His father, John, had passed away unexpectedly after pastoring the church for forty years. Joel had to immediately move from a behind-the-scenes job into the role of senior pastor, and it rocked his confidence. He regularly wondered if he could be as good as his dad. And he struggled with the belief that he had to give people what they were used to by preaching and leading in the same ways his dad had.

When I spoke with Joel about this recently, he recalled the feeling of inferiority he felt in those early months:

> When I first started preaching I thought I had to have a long opening text with forty support scriptures, like my dad. And during the week I thought I had to walk the halls and talk to everyone like he did. These things didn't suit my personality, though, and I struggled to find a balance between who I really was and who everyone expected me to be. Then one day I read Acts 13:36, where it says, "David had served God's purpose in his own generation," and it dawned on me that God was showing me I needed to be myself. It was like He lifted the words right out of Scripture and said, "Joel, your dad fulfilled *his* purpose for *his* generation; now go fulfill *your* purpose. They don't have to be the same!" What a relief that reality was for me! I was finally free to step into the role God had for me.[1]

> "It was like He lifted the words right out of Scripture and said, 'Joel, your dad fulfilled *his* purpose for *his* generation; now go fulfill *your* purpose.'"
>
> —JOEL OSTEEN

The Falwell brothers faced similar obstacles when their father, Jerry Falwell Sr., the senior pastor of Thomas Road Baptist Church and president of Liberty University, passed away unexpectedly. Suddenly they were thrust into very big shoes to fill. Jerry Jr. took over the university, and Jonathan took leadership of the church.

Jerry Jr. said, "I've not tried to do things exactly like Dad did. He was really stretched too thin. I had to break everyone of the notion that everything would be done just the way Dad did it. You have to be yourself. Always put 100 percent in, but don't try to copy other people, and don't try to be someone you are not. Do things your way."[2]

And Jonathan felt the same struggle to be like his dad as a pastor. "Because of who Dad was, people wanted me to speak [outside the church] or be involved in a lot of different things. It took time to get focused on the fact that God called me to be the pastor of a local church. And to be the pastor of a local church I wasn't called to speak at all these other events and conferences like Dad. . . . My dad was the pastor of a local church but far more than that. I saw that growing up. But God called me to a local church whether there are one hundred people or ten thousand. That's where my heart and focus needs to be."[3]

I'm sure both Falwell brothers had to accept the fact that they disappointed some people because they didn't do everything like their dad did. Joel gave some great advice about that when he said, "Be careful about listening to naysayers. You can't please everybody. Be who God has called you to be and take things in the direction He wants you to go. Some people didn't stand with me, but I had a strength from God to say 'You will not pigeon-hole me into being who you want me to be; I will be who God wants me to be.'"[4]

Be yourself and be true to who God has created you to be. It will save you and your people a lot of heartache down the road if you are authentic and transparent about your identity and gifts.

Always remember that God has called *you* to lead in this unique time in your organization's history. Never apologize for who you are; rather, stand confidently in your strengths, undergirded by God's enabling power.

3. Develop your vision

Naturally, as the senior pastor I had always been the vision-caster. When I led, I had a regular rhythm of spending time alone with God to determine what He was inspiring in my heart. Prayer and fasting have always been at the center of our process to discover God's will and make decisions at Christ Fellowship. Donna and I have consistently prayed together, coming together in oneness, to seek God's will for us and the church. And while things had changed frequently at Christ Fellowship over the years, the one thing that stayed consistent was that any new vision always fit within the framework of the broader mission of the church. It clearly reflected who we are, but it was always fresh in method and implementation.

When I passed the baton to Todd, I stressed that it was now his responsibility to listen to God for vision. Paul Osteen, Joel's brother, said Joel felt this same responsibility. He said Joel took time in God's presence to get the truly inspired vision so he could step out with confidence to declare it to the church. He said, "Nothing takes the place of getting in front of God yourself and letting Him birth what He wants to do in your church. Don't let committees give you the vision. God gives it."[5] This is so true. So as Todd prepared to take over leadership, he spent a lot of time praying for vision with Julie. They knew that the burden of responsibility to strategically plan for the church's future programs and initiatives would soon be theirs to carry. As they prayed and we made the transition, God faithfully gave them some clear directives.

After leading the charge as we moved to being a multisite church, Todd began to get a new vision in the year following the transition. He believed that God wanted us to launch two additional campuses that year. This would allow us to continue to grow under the steady influx of new people we were gaining, and to expand our ministry even further in the surrounding communities.

We had also been planting seeds of ministry in Belle Glade, a low-income rural town nearby. In lieu of summer camp, our teens had been going there each summer for a week of ministering to families and children—through sports camps, service projects, and vacation Bible school. After the transition, Todd felt strongly that our ministry needed to be an ongoing investment, not just one week out of the year, so he cast the vision for a Life Center that we would build and run to care for the children there, providing after-school programs for mentoring and tutoring. The Life Center was built in 2012 and continues to be a great resource to impact our neighbors for Christ.

Todd and Julie also had a calling to take a firm stand against human trafficking. Around the world, up to twenty-seven million people are living in slavery—that's more than at any other time in human history.[6] And Florida, our home state, is the number three state in the nation for the modern-day slave trade.[7] Todd's first step in involving Christ Fellowship in the cause was an initiative called Hope for Freedom, which raised awareness of the issue in our community and schools. Later, he discovered a vision for opening a faith-based, state-licensed safe house for young teenage girls who had been rescued and were in need of rehabilitation and counseling. He cast the vision to the congregation for this opportunity to bring light and healing to these victims. And I'm happy to say that Hope House was opened in October 2012 and is currently bringing restoration and healing to precious young girls.

These three initiatives represent the areas of vision in which God clearly led Todd in those early days of transition. I think it's important to note that none of them deviate, in any sense, from the overarching mission of the church. They are merely extensions of previous efforts. In fact, Todd made sure, when he talked about these new initiatives, to always point to the past. We already had five campuses when Todd and I made our transition, so campus development was central to our identity as a church and clearly understood in our culture. Our investment in Belle Glade was also understood and embraced long before Todd announced our intention to build a ministry center there. And as you already know, we had started Place of Hope in 2000 to care for children in the foster care system, so the safe house for those affected by human trafficking was a natural next step in caring for children in our community.

As the successor, assess the programs and practices your church or organization has focused on in the past. Then ask God for wisdom about how you can build on those things in the future. Whenever you can link the vision God has given you to the past foundations of the ministry, you will more easily help your people see the purpose and value of the decisions you are making for the organization.

Jerry Falwell Jr. understands this well. He said, "Our goal for Liberty is to be the first major American university that achieves everything academically and athletically that all the secular universities do while staying true to our Christian mission. . . . This was Dad's vision from Liberty's beginnings. I talk over and over about his vision and our total commitment to that vision."[8] Reiterating the mission your organization was built on when casting new vision will always create momentum and enthusiasm.

His brother Jonathan agrees. "God wants to assure us that His promises and provision are for us in this generation, at this time, just as they were in the time of our ancestors. He wants to give us a brand-new vision that, while connected to the past, will carry us into the future."[9] Leaders will always honor the legacy and kingdom work of the past while leaning in to God for new vision for the future.

4. Implement change slowly

As the successor, you may have some terrific insights and a vision from God about how to move the organization forward, but you need to remember that just because you are pregnant with ideas, it doesn't mean you should give birth to them tomorrow! Bringing something to life takes time. You have to "count the cost of changes" that you want to implement, as my friend Joel Osteen would say.[10]

In my interview with Bob and Rob Hoskins of OneHope, I asked them if they had any advice for incoming leaders. Rob was quick to say that he feels it's really important to champion the initiatives your predecessor set in motion before you took over. He said, "Ride that healthy horse. My predecessor built a great organization so the greatest thing I can do to enhance my leadership is to honor that person by not changing things too quickly. I might have my ideas where I want to see things five years from now, but I'm going to walk carefully and slowly to implement change. Doing anything else dishonors his leadership and methodology."[11]

And along with the potential of dishonoring your predecessor and your history as an organization, you also run the risk of hurting your people when you make changes too fast. When I interviewed Dave Stone about how he went about making changes after taking over for Bob Russell at Southeast Christian, he said:

> I underestimated how the older constituents would have a hard time adjusting to the changes I made. If I had it to do over again, I would have bent over backwards in that first year to try to reassure them that everything would be okay. It's tough when you follow someone who has been there for forty years and has grown the church from one hundred attendees to eighteen thousand. He had the track record and credibility to make whatever changes he wanted. I was only forty-five when I took over, and even though I had the blessing of the outgoing guy, for many it still felt like dad had turned the keys over to a sixteen-year-old reckless kid.[12]

Some things will naturally change as soon as you take over leadership, but there are many things that can wait till you've established yourself. You have to give people time to adjust to you. Give them time to feel secure about your love for them before you introduce a new set of ideas and programs. You have to communicate and help your people understand over time the what, why, how, and when for the changes you want to make, so that they buy into your goals and agenda.

I would strongly suggest you go slowly when making changes to programs and ministries within your church. Spend time getting to know and respect your people and the programs in which they are invested. Be extra sensitive and cautious about discontinuing programs that reflect the DNA of your church family.

My friend Larry Stockstill advises successors not to change too much at once. Start by making cosmetic changes first; then add to or modify existing programs, before proposing new programs and vision.[13] When Larry's son Jonathan took over as senior pastor at Bethany World Prayer Center, Jonathan's first desire was to propose a name change for the church. Larry advised him not to make such a big change until he had earned relational assets with the people.

Mike Erre, who was Chuck Swindoll's successor at First Evangelical Free Church in Fullerton, California, took over as leader of a large constituency of older congregants. He learned quickly how important it was to initiate change cautiously and judiciously. He equates it to building docks. There is value in keeping the old docks—working programs that still bring value and give honor to the older generations in the church. You just have to build new docks beside the old ones to support them. This will provide unity and encourage intergenerational ministry.[14]

Jerry Falwell Jr. feels the same. He said, "Some have the tendency to be too steeped in tradition and the past. Dad would say you have to change with the times; you have to adapt to new methods. But don't be mistaken; there has to be a balance."[15] And his brother agrees. "This isn't change for the sake of change. . . . We want to reach every available person, at every available time, using every available method . . . so we have to make a change here."[16]

American inventor Charles Kettering said, "If you have always done it that way, it is probably wrong."[17] It's important to evaluate why and how you do what you do to make sure you are being relevant to the generation you are reaching, while remaining true to the mission and core values of your organization. You just have to make the changes slowly and thoughtfully. As Joel Osteen put it, "Turn the ship slowly."[18] Prayerfully evaluate what you believe needs to be changed and do everything you can to communicate it at the right time. Keep clarifying your purpose for the change, explaining how it will help you better achieve your mission so you can be effective in the kingdom.

5. Work diligently to earn trust and credibility

Jason Bolin, who took over as senior pastor at Trinity Chapel in Powder Springs, Georgia, after his father's moral failure, understands well the need to earn respect and trust before making changes. During the Leadership Network simulcast on transitions, he said, "Build key relationships in the church. Don't assume you have trust. What you have initially is love until trust is earned."[19] That is a powerful reality! Your people may love you, especially if they've gotten to know you over the years in a supporting role, but it's important to remember that you have to earn your credibility as their leader over time.

> DON'T ASSUME YOU HAVE TRUST.
> WHAT YOU HAVE INITIALLY IS LOVE
> UNTIL TRUST IS EARNED.

Pastor Bryan Carter of Concord Church in Dallas, Texas, said, "New leaders must be patient. It takes time to earn credibility. You may be a pastor in 'title,' but you are not yet a pastor in 'position.'"[20] It takes time, but it's a fact that credibility earns trust; and when you have the trust of your people, you have room to implement change or try new things. People then are so much more receptive to your ideas and willing to help you make them happen.

One way you can work on building your credibility is to be intentional during your first ninety days to deliver your best and most inspiring messages from the pulpit. As Gene Appel, senior pastor of Anaheim, California's, Eastside Church, said at the Leadership Network Conference, "When you take over as a leader, so much hits your plate at once. The one thing you cannot afford to neglect is your prep time to deliver the Word. It's the number one evaluator to your people; and it's where you build your credibility the most."[21] This is where your people learn your heart and the platform for your vision. It's imperative that you focus on your heavy responsibility to deliver the Word effectively. One way you can do this well is by initially preaching shorter, more impactful messages. Don't try to throw in every Greek word or theological lesson you've learned in seminary. This is not the time for that. Just spend time praying about what your church family needs and do your best to meet those needs while casting vision for your role as their leader. This will build a foundation of trust and credibility faster than anything else you can do or plan for in directing your leadership.

6. Build your own team gradually

Typically, when a new coach takes over a sports team, the old coaching staff is released so that the new coach can select his or her own. This allows the new person to bring in staff members with whom he already has a relationship and loyalty so he can make sure he has the strongest staff to lead the team to victory.

In the church, as you might imagine, this isn't usually the case. Successors in churches will usually have to work with the existing team present at the time of their transition. You can't just come in and kick everybody out. That would hardly endear your staff or congregation to you.

I would suggest, for at least the first year of your leadership, that you not make a lot of major staffing changes in the key positions of your organization. Of course, if you were previously a part of the team you will now be leading, it is important that you select someone, either from within the organization or outside it, who can take your previous role and support your leadership. You may even find, as Todd did, that you will end up filling multiple positions upon your transition.

Once Todd knew the exchange between us was getting closer, he recognized that he would have to transition out of his own role as executive pastor. At that point, he sat down and assessed which of his responsibilities would need to be passed on to a successor. What he discovered was that he had been functioning for quite some time in a number of roles. Overseeing the day-to-day operations and the various ministries of the church was a huge job, but to add to that, he also led our efforts to be a multisite church. There were so many facets to each of those roles, and they were quite different from one another. As he considered the job description for executive pastor, he knew he needed to make some adjustments or he would surely overwhelm his own successor.

He ended up splitting his prior responsibilities into two distinct jobs—a director of ministry and a director of multisite, and hired two people who had experience in those areas. He restructured a few existing roles on his leadership team as well. Nothing major changed from an outsider's perspective, except maybe titles. He kept the team intact, for the most part. This gave everyone on the team and in our church family a sense of security—that things wouldn't change that drastically from a staffing perspective. Since the staff empowers the congregation to do ministry in the church, bringing in a lot of new staff could have really unsettled people.

Don't be discouraged if it takes some time to build a strong team around you. It will require a lot of investment on your part to gain the trust and loyalty of your team. This is normal; but it will come with time and experience.

Dave Stone of Southeastern Christian Church and his predecessor, Bob Russell, had selected an additional, younger preacher to join their team long before Dave took over as senior pastor. Kyle Idleman has worked under Dave for many years, and one of the things Kyle did when Dave took over was write him a letter. In it he said, "I just want you to know I will be loyal to you. If there are ever any problems between you and me that could harm the body of Christ, I will graciously bow out. That won't ever be a problem you will have to worry about." You need to have people around you who will be loyal to your leadership and be sold out to the kingdom vision and purpose God gives you. Let your staff know what you expect from them and what they can expect from you. Honor begets honor. Loyalty begets loyalty. Always model for your staff what you expect in return.

Obviously you may not have the benefit of already being on the staff or even a member of the church for which you are taking over leadership. You may have been recruited for this role and are coming in fresh. If that's the case, it's even more important that you keep the existing team intact until you have been there for some time. You need a strong core to help you acclimate to your new role and teach you how the organization functions. The existing team will be your backbone, especially in those early months.

And if that's you, I would suggest meeting with your directors or ministry leaders as soon as possible to garner their help and partnership as you get started together. Create covenants that clearly communicate the things you are striving for and the ways you will protect one another.

Jonathan Falwell said that because there had been no formal plan for succession, he had never led their staff in any capacity before his father's death. So just days before he took over as senior pastor, his new followers had been his peers. Because of this, he embraced more of a team approach to casting vision and leading the ministry of the church during the first year. He said, "Over a period of a year or two, I then transitioned away from leaning on them to leading them."[22]

You definitely need to rely on the existing team and your leadership board to help you navigate new waters. They have been there. They know how things have been done in the past. They know what has and has not worked. They will have helpful insights and opinions about what can and cannot be changed right away. Lean in to this team as you get adjusted.

Once you have led for some time, it's important to build your own team. You have to have the right people around you who will accommodate your strengths and shore up your weaknesses. Once you get some experience and really have a grip on the vision God has for you and the organization moving forward, you need to make sure you have the right people to carry it out. This might mean making some tough calls along the way. You may have some people who have served faithfully for many years under your predecessor, but don't fit well in that role under your leadership. Tread lightly but bravely in those circumstances. Prayerfully consider where else they might fit, because you never want to let eagles go—those who are hardworking and loyal to the Lord's work in your organization. Even if you can't fit them on your staff or in a position of leadership moving forward, determine and embrace their skills and gifting for some role in the body. Then, after you have given this some thought and prayer, meet with them and explain the situation and how you see things, making sure you affirm their strengths and thank them for their contribution. This is never easy, but it is a reality of leading.

Joel Osteen was faced with some difficulty when he started putting his own team together.

> My personality was such that I never wanted to hurt anyone's feelings or deal with confrontation, but I knew that in order for us to be where we were supposed to be, I had to grow out of that. It was clear that there were some people in positions going in directions I knew we weren't going. It was really difficult for me to have those discussions with people I loved. They were so loyal, but I knew they weren't going to be able to fulfill the needs of the role as I saw it in the future. There came a point when I had to ask myself if keeping everything seemingly perfect and avoiding hurt feelings would be worth not fulfilling the destiny God had called us towards. It was hard to do, but in hindsight, it was the right thing to do and God helped us all.[23]

Ministry is hard work; don't get me wrong! It is incredibly rewarding work, but undoubtedly there is a huge price to be paid. You can't do it alone; surround yourself with a team that will stand by you so you can fulfill the calling God has given you.

7. Keep an open door to your predecessor

Your greatest storehouse of wisdom and understanding in the organization is your predecessor. He knows better than anyone what you are going through in your new role.

> YOUR GREATEST STOREHOUSE OF
> WISDOM AND UNDERSTANDING . . .
> IS YOUR PREDECESSOR.

Do what you can to reach out to him and seek his counsel. If you are new to your church or organization, your predecessor will be especially helpful in explaining why certain decisions had been made that you are now trying to manage or adapt under your leadership. He will provide some historical context for how and why things were done in the past.

Your predecessor will also help point out and provide you with insight about the key influencers in the church and how to best engage them for ministry under your leadership. One of the greatest things you can do with a key influencer is understand not only what value he will bring to you and the organization, but what value you can add to his personal life. Your predecessor will know some of the things that have been helpful in the past and can help you understand how you can pour into key influencers' lives and have lasting impact as their leader.

Your predecessor will also know what pitfalls to avoid and can help you make sure you don't make any unnecessary rookie mistakes as a new leader. Take advantage of whatever relationship your predecessor is willing to have with you. Consider him a valuable mentor and prioritize the relationship.

I know it's a new day and God has given you a new vision, but it's always a smart thing to seek the counsel of the one who has lived in the land you are now inhabiting.

I'm so thankful I get to encourage Todd and help him think through the decisions he has to make for the welfare of Christ Fellowship. I try to meet with him weekly for a formal, closed-door meeting where he can hash out things with me and glean my insights on the ministry we both love. I understand well what he's going through and can sympathize with some of the harder aspects of doing ministry. And I know him well, so I'm able to affirm him and help him keep perspective. I can hold his arms up when he's weak and draw on his strengths to get him going again. I always try to be there when he needs me to pray with him and offer him wisdom from someone who has walked in his shoes.

If you can set up regular meetings with your predecessor, even by video chat or phone if you can't meet in person, it will help you tremendously.

Of course, you might be a successor who doesn't have access to your predecessor, for any number of reasons. In your situation, it becomes very important for you to find a pastor of a different church whom you can ask to mentor you. Spending time with someone who has weathered a few more seasons than you have will offer you guidance and encouragement.

8. Honor the past

The fact that you are a successor means you are following someone else. Make sure you acknowledge that regularly and always say and do things that demonstrate honor for the past leader and his or her leadership.

Isaac Newton said, "If I have seen farther than others, it is because I was standing on the shoulders of giants."[24] I think it's important to keep that in mind, because it keeps you humble and grounded. It also helps your people stay connected to God's faithfulness in the legacy of the leaders before you. This has been especially important at Christ Fellowship since we have evolved into a multisite megachurch. Whenever possible, Todd points back with gratitude to our foundation to provide context for where we've been in light of where we are going. It creates unity, making a large church much smaller and more like a family.

Along with regularly communicating honor for your predecessor, I would encourage you to look for practical ways to physically honor him or her. Jim Garlow, who was John Maxwell's successor at Skyline, named buildings after John and John's predecessor, Pastor Orval Butcher, to honor the past leadership and keep their impact and legacy constantly before the people.[25]

Bob Russell shared in his book *Transitions* that before he passed the baton to Dave Stone, his community held a leaders' breakfast where people were given a chance to share what the ministry at Southeast Christian meant to them. The women's ministry held a special luncheon in honor of Bob's wife, Judy. And in Bob's final worship service, video testimonies were given by a variety of people in the church, recalling shared experiences and expressing their gratitude. Bob would be the first to tell you that these special touches honored and blessed him.

A special service was held at Christ Fellowship before Todd and I officially exchanged the baton. During the service, our elders publicly thanked Donna and me for our years of leadership, and we celebrated as a church family all weekend long.

These mile markers are important for you and your people.

And let me just say that when you honor your predecessor, you will always endear your people to your heart. John Maxwell wisely said when he succeeded Orval Butcher, "The quickest way for my people to love me was to love the man who loved them for twenty-seven years."[26]

> ## MILE MARKERS ARE IMPORTANT
> ## FOR YOU AND YOUR PEOPLE.

Remember that your people have a relationship investment in your predecessor. He was the one who dedicated their babies, united them in marriage, and stood by them at the graveside of their loved ones. When you constantly elevate your predecessor and honor him with your words and deeds, the people will eventually transfer that relationship and loyalty to you.

9. Keep a balanced perspective

Former president Franklin Delano Roosevelt once said, "It's a terrible thing to look over your shoulder when you are trying to lead and find no one there."[27] The reality is that not everyone is going to embrace you. Some will struggle too much through the transition to accept the changes. Some will compare you to your predecessor too much and won't believe in you. Because of this reality, you have to keep things in perspective. You simply won't win everyone's heart. And that has to be okay. Remember this: you aren't called to lead people who aren't there. Focus your

attention and affections on the people who stay and the new people who will come.

Previously I told you the story about how discouraged Dave
Stone was when he took over for Bob Russell. A thousand people
left in Dave's first eighteen months as lead pastor. It really hurt his
confidence and focus because he felt as though losing anyone was
a failure. Later when he finally talked with Bob, Bob told him to
focus on the seventeen thousand who were still there.

And it's hard to believe anyone would have left Lakewood
Church when Joel took over. I've never met a more sincere and
sweet-spirited man of God than Joel. And yet, the reality is that
some people didn't stay. His brother Paul remarked, "For every
one person who left, we blessed them as they went and believed
God would bring twenty to replace them."[28] And history shows
that God did indeed multiply their church family and continues
to pour His favor out on their ministry.

Another thing to keep in perspective is that what you are
embarking on is hard work. You need to acknowledge that there
will be days when you will want to give up. It's in those times
that you need to lean in to God, reflect on your calling, and press
through the tough times.

Dave Stone told me about an idea (or coping mechanism) he
shared with his wife when he succeeded Bob Russell. He told
her, "I am going to put five hundred marbles in an aquarium and
keep it in my office. I will take out one marble each day for a
year and a half. If, after I have 'lost all my marbles,' I find that
I'm still not fit to do this and I feel like I need to step down, I
will. At least I'll know in my heart that I gave it my best." By the

end of those five hundred days, God had indeed taken him on a difficult prayer journey, moving him from fear to faith so he would be more dependent on Him. Dave would tell you that he is extremely happy and fulfilled now in his job, but he would just as quickly tell you he wouldn't have gotten to that place without walking through the valley.

Sometimes we have to trudge through the valleys with God so we learn to put our faith and reliance completely in Him. And trust me when I say, that's the only way to lead effectively—from a place of submission to and reliance upon God. He alone is our high tower and our mighty Deliverer. He alone will carry you through the dark days of trial and discouragement. He is your Helper. Lean in to all He has for you, and He will lead you through the tough days of ministry into the blessings of serving the King of your heart.

And the last thing I would suggest you keep in balanced perspective is the fact that you don't have to be great right out of the gate, but you do need to strive to be good. Your predecessor may have been a great leader in your organization when he made his transition. You are coming in at the bottom and probably feel that you have a lot to prove. Many successors I've spoken with said they felt as though they had to do something substantial to prove their worth and credibility.

> SOW INTO THE SEEDS OF GREATNESS ALREADY EXISTING IN THE ORGANIZATION.

But a better strategy is to sow into the seeds of greatness already existing in the organization. Build on top of what is already considered the great aspects of the existing programs started and managed by your predecessor. When you do that, your leadership grows and your level of respect and credibility grows exponentially.

When I interviewed John Maxwell for this project he talked specifically about this very inclination of new leaders. He said:

> So many times when guys come in they say, "I've gotta make my mark." But I came to realize that the quickest way for me to succeed as a follower of someone else was to make sure that the "marks" he made would become greater. And when people realized that I wasn't trying to take anything away from the founder they let me do what I wanted. But when you as the successor start injecting what you want into the church, the first thing that becomes to the people is a threat, and they say, "Wait a minute. Pastor 'So Great' didn't do that! He was the pastor here for twenty-five years and he never did that. Why does Pastor 'Not So Great' want to do that?" I just learned that if the successor would just concentrate during the first year or two on making the success of the founder even greater, then they can move forward and do what they want. When people are convinced that you love them and you aren't trying to "make your mark," they are going to love you and let you lead.[29]

———

I hope these tips are helpful to you as you prepare to step into the role God has for you. Do your best to think through each one and consider where you need to make improvements before you get too far down the pike. If it isn't time yet for your transition to take place, be patient. Wait on God to lead on your behalf at the right time. And when it is time, be yourself. Remember that you have been chosen for this position because of the leader *you* are. Stand up and lean in to your strengths, trusting God to shore up your weaknesses and surround you with the people you need to fulfill the vision He has given you after you've diligently spent time seeking His heart.

Go about making changes slowly and cautiously, being sensitive to the people around you and their part in God's kingdom work. Be honoring and work diligently to earn the trust and credibility you need to make those changes. And always keep your door open to your predecessor. Be humble and teachable. Honor the past, remembering that you are standing on the shoulders of those who have gone before you. And finally, ask God to help you keep the right perspective and motives each day.

I know God will be faithful to carry you through your transition as you walk humbly with Him in the lead and seek to do His will. May God bless you and guide you into greater days ahead for His kingdom's sake.

TIPS FOR RUNNERS ENTERING THE EXCHANGE ZONE

Positioning Others for Success

A winner knows how much he still has to learn, even
when he is considered an expert by others.

—SYDNEY HARRIS[1]

As an old football coach, I became used to evaluating every
aspect of our team's performance. Every practice was followed by a staff meeting. There, we evaluated not only how the
players were performing but also how we as coaches were performing. We asked how our organizational structure was that day
and whether our drills accomplished the end results needed.

Coaches plan down to the minute for every practice scheduled
so they make sure they get the most out of their time together as
a team. They constantly evaluate effort, skill development, and
team chemistry of both individuals and team units, such as how a
set of four defensive backs moves and plays together; and the same
goes for the offensive backfield. Some linemen just read and play
off certain players better than others.

Our biggest evaluations took place after games. We would start by breaking down game film. By Sunday afternoon we had evaluated our players' performance, our game plan execution, and the calls on both sides of the ball, as well as any weaknesses we needed to work on to face our next opponent. Evaluation was a huge part of my role as a coach because it was the key to making the changes necessary for victory.

ELEVEN TIPS FOR HANDING OFF THE BATON WELL

As a pastor, I still constantly evaluate. It has been three years since our transition at Christ Fellowship, and I still ask myself if there was anything I could have done better. My ultimate goal was to set up the organization and Todd for success when he eventually took over as lead pastor. As his dad, I naturally wanted Todd to thrive. But in addition, I knew that part of my own legacy would be contingent upon my preparation of Todd, our staff, and our church family for the transition and on my ability to leave well.

With these goals in mind, I gave considerable thought to what I did well and what I could have improved along with the questions that have come up in the process of counseling other outgoing pastors. Accordingly, I put together a few universal tips to share that I hope will prove helpful to you as you make your own transition.

1. Make tough calls before the exchange

I would highly suggest that before you hand off the baton of leadership to your successor, you make any tough calls that are needed. For example, if there are staff or board member changes that you know need to take place but have been put off for one reason or another, handle those. Make the team that will support your successor as strong as possible.

Maybe there are budget cuts that should be made in order to put your successor in a better position to lead from a place of freedom. If so, you need to sit down with your accounting team and the ministry teams affected by the potential cuts and take care of them before you leave.

No one wants to inherit a mess! Don't leave your successor with a bunch of issues to deal with right off the bat. Instead, do whatever is in your power to position him to walk on the smoothest possible path. Again, simply think of how you would want to step into your role and do what you can to make sure that happens for your successor.

2. Make yourself available beyond the exchange zone

I've already mentioned that it may not be beneficial for you to stay on the team or even at the same church after the transition, but I would challenge you to do whatever it takes to make yourself available to your successor after the exchange is officially made.

As I shared before, Bob Russell chose to stay away for a year after handing the leadership baton to Dave Stone. There were positives that came from Bob humbly staying away for a stretch. But in retrospect, Dave wishes he had reached out to Bob and discussed his (Dave's) fears and challenges.

Don't underestimate how valuable your availability is to your successor. Everyone needs someone to get behind them and rally them through the challenges of ministry. But you need to be the initiator here. Most successors won't want to bother their predecessors with things they think they have to figure out on their own. You can alleviate this by simply being available to talk, and validating your successor's challenges by bringing up familiar experiences that you had when you were in his shoes.

You probably know as well as I do that leadership can be a lonely road. Don't let your successor go it alone. Let him know you are ready and able to listen and offer counsel whenever he needs it.

Perhaps having a conversation with your successor in which you tell him you are available whenever he needs you is as simple as it needs to be. Maybe you need to offer a monthly luncheon or golf outing to touch base and discuss whatever is on your successor's heart. Maybe you just need to text him periodically to check in and ask how things are going. Whatever works, works. Just make yourself available to mentor your successor in a non-threatening or imposing manner.

3. Ask your key leaders to be loyal to your successor during the transition

It's very important to challenge your staff and other key leaders to stay with the new leader to help bring stability to the organization during your transition. At the time of our transition at Christ Fellowship, I asked our board of elders, staff, ministry leaders, and congregation to fully get behind and support Todd as our leader. I requested that they give him the same loyalty and love that they had given me during my years as their leader.

John Maxwell did this at Skyline when he left as well. He asked his core leaders to make a three-year commitment to his successor, Jim Garlow. In our interview he said, "One of the first things I did that helped the church tremendously was to go to my core leaders when I was preparing to leave and say, 'I am asking one thing of you. If you value what I've done in developing you as a leader and disciple of Christ, I am asking you for payback. Stay with the church for three years for me. If after three years, you want to go to another church, go to another church. But I want you to make this new pastor a success, and his success will be greatly determined by your spirit and attitude to help him and stand by him for the next three years."[2]

Compassion International president and CEO Wess Stafford did this for his successor, Jim Mellado, when he was preparing for his retirement. He wrote a letter to all their supporters to outline Jim's credibility and ask them to pray and support their transition. Then, for the last nine months, they traveled to events together where Wess has introduced Jim to the world. In doing so, Wess has essentially built an infrastructure that supports not only his successor but also the longevity of Compassion International's reach.

Whenever you can leverage the influence and impact you've had with your people, you ought to do so for the sake of your successor. Asking your influencers to remain at the church to support the new guy will provide some added security to the organization's health during that fragile time of transition, because influencers lead and support the ministries of the church. And even more importantly, their presence and commitment will boost the morale of your successor as he tries to find his footing to lead well.

4. Invite your successor into your network

As you expand your network and continue to build your relationships with people of influence, invite your successor into your inner circle. When I think back on the connections I've made through introductions from others, I can see clearly how those connections took us from where we were as a church back then to the church we are today. One such relationship was with Roger Breland, the founder of the Christian band Truth, which was popular from the 1970s through the 1990s. He introduced me to Dr. Jay Strack, the founder of Student Leadership University, which trains middle and high school students in their leadership skills. And Jay introduced me to world-renowned leadership guru John Maxwell, who has become a good friend.

As my relationship with John grew through the years, he pulled me into his circle of influence and gave me credibility with his peers. As a result, I have had the privilege of meeting and partnering with some of the greatest global leaders in ministry. The impact of those relationships is immeasurable because they have added such value to my life and leadership.

I can personally attest to the fact that important introductions like these are a priceless gift that will keep on giving to your successor for years to come. And further, it's a way to continue to indirectly add value to the ministry that you invested in for years. Always look for opportunities to add value to your successor, and ultimately the organization, by leveraging the relationships you've benefitted from in the past for your successor's future.

5. Be your successor's number one advocate

Leaders are lifters of others, so you should always look for ways to honor and affirm your successor, both publicly and privately. Whether you agree with every new idea and initiative your successor undertakes or not, never speak negatively about his or her decisions in public. If you have real concerns with genuine motives, approach your successor in private to share them. One of the greatest gifts you can give to the one who comes after you is your public support.

> ## LEADERS ARE LIFTERS OF OTHERS.

Further, never underestimate the power of your influence after you step away from your leadership position in your church. Never forget that no matter where you are, what you say about your successor will always find its way back home to him or her in some conversation with a mutual friend. Wherever I travel and with whomever I talk, I always make sure I share all the positives about the job that Todd is doing in leading Christ Fellowship. I do this because I want to celebrate what's taking place, and I want him to hear from others how I honor and celebrate his leadership.

The apostle Paul told us that we need to think on things of good report (Phil. 4:8). And you and I both know that what we think about directly influences the things we say. Accordingly, I am committed to looking constantly for the good things happening in the ministry of Christ Fellowship so that I can be a bearer of good news—of the good things God is doing through others.

In addition to speaking well of your successor, I firmly believe you need to find ways to directly encourage him in his efforts to lead. Encouragement is oxygen to the soul, particularly during trying times. Your successor is stepping into a huge role, as you well know. You know the ups and downs and the dry seasons. Anticipate those times, and reach out with an encouraging word. I would suggest you even put a reminder on your calendar to send him a note at least once a month. I assure you it will never go unnoticed or unappreciated! I still have encouraging notes tucked away in a drawer that I go back through and reread in the challenging times.

David Shibley did this for his son Jonathan when he first took over as president of Global Advance. He said, "I wrote several personal letters on different nuances of presiding over a missions ministry. Also, as is the custom of US presidents, I left a very special letter in his desk for him to unseal and read on the first day of his presidency."[3] I am confident that Jonathan rereads those special letters just as I read mine. Take the time to write them because I think it will mean the world to your successor to hear from someone who understands his struggles intimately and can encourage him in his leadership.

6. Get your financial situation in order

As I alluded to in chapter 2, the financial picture for the future of a leader who has served for a long time with the church can be a sensitive area to address. Some boards make preparations for their pastors in anticipation of setting up great retirement plans. Sadly, though, many do not.

In my own case, because I was a founding pastor feeling tremendous responsibility for the financial future of my church, I often didn't accept any extra money for my own future planning and instead channeled anything extra to the needs of the ministry at that time. Christ Fellowship has experienced major growth for the last thirty years, so ministry needs always tended to outpace giving. Accordingly, intentionally setting aside funds for the future never got my attention.

As I neared the time to pass the leadership baton to Todd, John C. Maxwell approached me and asked if our board had prepared to take care of me financially after the transition. Unbeknownst to me, our board had had numerous discussions about this very matter with Todd. They established a financial plan that will adjust as my involvement shifts and changes in the future.

A pastor and good friend of mine in one of the nation's larger churches has a really healthy relationship with his board. Together, they have a plan for his transition, ten years in advance of the actual time it will take place. And one of the things they have created is a "Rabbi trust" where they put money away in a special account that can earn interest and eventually be used to support their outgoing pastors. Another great church has established a deferred compensation plan for their pastor's retirement. I thought these were great ideas for all of us to learn from. Explore the options! There are plenty of ways to approach it, but the key is having these important conversations with your board.

No one wants to approach this conversation from a position of entitlement to such compensation, but at the same time I'm convinced that these conversations must take place, particularly as leaders planning for our next assignment. One way you can approach this conversation tactfully is through an advocate who can approach the board on your behalf, as John was willing to do for me if our board hadn't already set a plan in motion. Remember, this is not only helping to secure your future; it will help set the tone for how all the future leaders of your organization will be cared for in the years to come.

7. Stay relevant

I think it's really important for you to stay relevant and engaged with the people you once related to in ministry. A lot of guys I know pulled back from their relationships with other pastors and leaders after their transition. They stopped hanging out with those they had associated with previously, because they don't feel as though they have anything in common anymore.

This is a mistake. There is no greater time of needing those friendships and relationships than during a transition. You need to press in and engage those leaders in order to stay relevant and better able to relate to the upcoming generations of leaders. Those relationships will help you identify with the needs of younger leaders, so you know how to add value and connect on their level.

I can see how easy it would be to just pull out of the ministry scene and lose your sense of identity as a senior leader, but let me caution you that the enemy of your soul wants nothing more than to take you out of the game and make you ineffective. Don't let this happen. Find ways to connect, whether through speaking at or attending conferences, serving on boards or committees, or speaking at other churches in a guest capacity.

I have tried to do each of these things since our transition at Christ Fellowship. Along with my new responsibilities as president of EQUIP, I regularly attend and speak at conferences whenever I think I can add value or connect with other Christian leaders to help grow and expand the kingdom of God. I also serve on other churches' advisory boards and other nonprofit committees so I can continue to learn and network. And I regularly speak at other churches to give my pastor friends a break or for special events. In my experience, many pastors especially appreciate when a trusted guest can come and talk to their congregations on more challenging topics like stewardship. But whatever the topic may be, I always want to remain relevant and available so God can continue to use me for His glory.

8. Adopt spiritual sons

Now that your transition has given you some extra time, I would suggest you make every effort to seek out spiritual sons whom you can mentor as they prepare for their next steps in ministry as I mentioned earlier in chapter 4. If you look closely enough, you'll find a few who would really benefit from you taking the time to sow into them and help them develop their strengths. And of course this applies to women as well. If you are a woman, you should be "adopting" spiritual daughters.

The number one question I'm asked since I turned the leadership over to Todd is, "Will you mentor me?" Whenever I speak at conferences, I always get a handful of guys who approach me with that question. They all want a spiritual father to come alongside them and stir up their gifts and help them get to the next level. Many admittedly didn't have earthly fathers who encouraged them or validated them. Accordingly, I feel it is my job to stand in the gap and be the spiritual dad they desperately long for and need as they grow in their leadership.

I give them healthy affection and call them "son," so they know just how much I love them. I also always look for ways to draw out their strengths and help validate what I see in them. I want them to walk away from time with me feeling affirmed and valued, clearly knowing how great I think they are and what an asset they are to the kingdom of God.

I also do my best to help stabilize them in storms. A young man who is like a son to me got into an inappropriate relationship with a member of his church. As a result, he had to resign. I knew he felt a great deal of shame and remorse, and probably feared being transparent with those of us who love him and have invested in him as a young leader. But I wanted to make sure he knew he was still my spiritual son, and nothing he could do would change that. When we got together next, I told him I loved him and that I was so proud of him for taking steps to make restitution and grow through it. Sons need to know you will stick by them and hold them up in the hard times.

Wherever I go, I "adopt" sons, even internationally. A couple years ago I was in the Middle East and met a young political leader who served us the entire time we were there. At the end of our time together I told him I thought of him as a son and wanted to "adopt" him as a son. His eyes lit up as we embraced and said our good-byes. A few months later, he contacted me and said he would be traveling in the States and really wanted to spend time with his "dad." We enjoyed our time together and continue to keep in touch. In fact, in every e-mail I receive from him, he greets me as "Dad."

> NEVER UNDERESTIMATE THE VALUE YOU CAN ADD TO THE NEXT GENERATION IN THE MINISTRY.

Never underestimate the value you can add to the next generation in the ministry. They need your loving investment in their lives; and they need the wisdom and experience you can provide. Now is the time to share it. This new season after the transition is the perfect time to seek out and raise up the spiritual sons around you.

Searching for our place in the days after a transition can be difficult. Let me challenge you to find new purpose in investing in others. I assure you, there will never be a void in your ministry life if you raise up spiritual sons, because there will always be a demand for you as a father. It's a role that will never change.

Always put yourself in positions to add value to the younger generation of young men rising up to take their place in ministry. Don't shy away when you get asked the question, "Will you mentor me?" God can use the things you've experienced to help a lot of other men if you will simply be available.

9. Start writing

I had already written three books before I transitioned out of my senior leadership role. The ability to write is a great practice to have, but I never truly realized how important it was until John Maxwell and I had a conversation after the transition, during which he said, "Tom, books *are* your legacy. You get to leave the wisdom you want to share for future generations. They will be your voice when you are gone." And he was right. I know I would give anything to have my grandfather's wisdom recorded in a book to read and reread through the years.

I used to think books were only written by the experts or the innovators. Now I know books are written by men and women who want to preserve the lessons and insights of their generation for those yet to come. And look: if you've been in ministry for a while, you have learned some lessons and insights along the way! Don't underestimate the value of preserving them for others.

Right now I'm also in the process of writing the history of the first thirty years of ministry at Christ Fellowship with my wife, Donna. We have wanted to do this for a long time, but never slowed down long enough to record our thoughts. Now, in this new season, we are making time.

We've always been asked to share the stories of how we grew from a small group in our home to hosting more than ninety thousand people on our campuses this past Easter. But this question is even more common in the time since the transition. A lot happened along the journey that other people can learn from. I want the other book that I'm writing to be a primer of sorts that will help other churches both avoid some of our mistakes and embrace some of our victories. And I want the future leaders of Christ Fellowship to absorb our DNA as they understand the values and virtues that have undergirded our foundation for years.

We all have a story. We all have valuable lessons and insights that we've learned along the way. Perhaps you have a great sermon series that resulted in a lot of changed lives for eternity. Maybe you need to consider taking that content and turning it into a book that will continue to have impact long after you are gone.

Whatever the case may be, I would challenge you to pick up your pen and start recording your ideas, so you can have a voice long after God calls you to glory. The times change so quickly, but truth remains. Let your words stand as markers of truth to light the path for those who will follow you.

10. Pray

> THE MOST IMPORTANT THING YOU CAN DO AS AN OUTGOING LEADER IS TO PRAY FOR YOUR SUCCESSOR.

The most important thing you can do as an outgoing leader is to pray for your successor. Pray daily for his wisdom, strength, and protection. Pray for his integrity. Pray for his marriage. Pray for an even greater harvest of people changed for eternity under his ministry. A couple of times a month, especially in the early months following the transition, text or otherwise contact your successor to let him know you are praying for him and ask if there is anything specific you can pray for. It will mean so much to your successor to know you are undergirding him in prayer.

11. Never retire

After "Will you mentor me?" the second most common question I've been asked since the transition is, "What are you doing now that you're retired?" My immediate response is always to laugh. Then I explain that I don't really believe in retirement, or at least not in the traditional sense.

As I explained earlier, I believe there is always something we can do in God's kingdom, no matter our age. I have had two great examples for me in my grandfather and the chairman of our board at Christ Fellowship, Dick Smith.

My grandfather empowered young leaders in the church far before he was ready to step down from leadership at his church, because he understood the transition process well. But he never stepped away from God's work entirely until his dying day. He always found a way to invest and sow seeds that long outlived him and still have impact today.

And Dick and his family were one of the original five families that met in our home when Christ Fellowship first started in 1984. He is an original board member who is now eighty-six years old and still serves, providing wisdom and care to our leadership team. His investment of his life has been so steadfast and faithful.

I want to be in a position to do the same. I want to run hard till Jesus carries me home, and so should you. Determine what's next for you and wake up each day with a clear sense of direction and purpose, knowing you are still a difference-maker in the kingdom.

———

I hope these tips are helpful as you prepare to make your transition out of your senior leadership position. My goal was to provide you with some guidance that would help make your transition easier, along with some advice that would help you set your successor up for success in his new role.

Transitions of this magnitude are difficult. There are so many changes and adjustments to make. However, I believe that if you focus on having a kingdom perspective on the necessity of having and implementing transition plans, you will leave behind a legacy of responsibility and honor. People will see that you put the health of the organization and what's best for your successor before yourself. And that will say so much about you as a leader and your priorities for the church.

In addition to managing your perspective about the transition, always look for ways to add value to your successor. Ask yourself what you can do to make his transition as tidy and easy as possible. If there are issues that need to be addressed before you hand off the baton, take care of them. Don't let anything linger that may cause unnecessary strife and added pressure to your successor in his early days of leadership.

Do whatever is necessary to make sure your successor knows you are available to him in the days, weeks, and months following the transition. Knowing you want to help him be his very best and reminding him that you have been where he is and can be a shoulder to lean on and a hand to guide him, will be a source of strength on tough days.

Be an encourager. Speak only positively of your successor in anyone else's presence. You won't agree with every decision he makes about every issue, but you need to support his leadership regardless. And whenever possible, speak highly of your successor, particularly in circles outside the church. Elevate the kingdom efforts he is making and celebrate the good things as often as possible, remembering that you are your successor's number one advocate.

Be prayerful and look for ways to be a faithful minister to the very end. Stand firm as an example for others to follow as they seek after Christ. I'm confident God will help you as you look for ways to help your successor and keep yourself available to Him to pour out until He calls you home.

RUNNING THROUGH STORMS

Leading Through Crisis-Driven Transitions

Every major difficulty you face in life is a fork in the road. You choose
which track you will head down, toward breakdown or breakthrough.

—JOHN C. MAXWELL[1]

I n his book *One Great Truth*, Jonathan Falwell recounts the events
of the day that proved to be the most difficult he had ever faced.
It was a beautiful spring morning in May when his mother, Macel,
called him and expressed concern that her husband, Jerry Falwell,
the senior pastor of Thomas Road Baptist Church and president
of Liberty University, had not shown up for a regularly scheduled meeting and couldn't be reached on his phone. Assuring his
mother that there was a good explanation and that everything was
fine, Jonathan called to see if his dad's assistant could verify his
father's whereabouts. She encouraged him to come to his father's
office, and immediately Jonathan knew something was wrong by
the wavering in her voice.

When he arrived, the scene was surreal, like something out of a movie. Chairs were overturned and medics were leaning over Dr. Falwell, trying to resuscitate him. Jonathan rushed to his father's side and knelt beside him, holding his hand as tears ran down his face. After long minutes of CPR, no one in the room looked hopeful. His dad, his friend, his mentor, his hero, was dying.

As they transported Dr. Falwell to the hospital in Lynchburg, Virginia, Jonathan asked the paramedics if anything had changed. There was no movement, no response on the monitors, and no positive remarks from the emergency crew. Once inside the emergency room, the efforts continued, but despite every possible procedure to lengthen his life, Dr. Falwell was gone.

In the days following Jerry Falwell's passing into glory, Jonathan struggled tremendously with what to do next. He said the pain of his loss gripped him like nothing he had ever experienced before, and the only thing that distracted him from his pain was the fear of what would happen now that his father was gone. He wasn't sure how he would face the church family where he had served as his dad's executive pastor for several years. He didn't know what he was going to say to bring them comfort or help them see a hope for the future. He didn't know who would be chosen to take over as their new leader. He didn't even know how to handle his own heartache and confusion. The Falwells and the church family were in crisis.[2]

Jerry Falwell hadn't done much transition planning with Jonathan or the team at Thomas Road Baptist Church. There was no written plan, and nothing had been spoken about before his death, because, as Jonathan put it, "He thought he'd live till he was a hundred."[3] So in the wake of his sudden death, Jonathan and the staff had no clear plan for who would take over. Dr. Falwell had been pastor of Thomas Road for more than fifty years. So the sudden loss was devastating for everyone.

In contrast, an unofficial plan had been made at Liberty University for the transition of his other son, Jerry. Neither Jerry Sr. nor Jerry Jr. had discussed it in anything other than general terms. And they only referred to it as something way down the road, because Dr. Falwell was afraid it would upset the family to discuss it. In 2003, Dr. Falwell had asked the board of the university to appoint Jerry Jr. as vice chancellor. It was written into the by-laws that in the case of Jerry Sr.'s death, Jerry Jr. would take over the leadership of the university. The intended transition was much clearer at Liberty than at Thomas Road, but while Jerry Sr. and Jerry Jr. had talked privately about how the transition would unfold, Dr. Falwell decided not to share those detailed discussions with other family members, who might have been alarmed that he was concerned about his health.

No other time is more important to have a transition plan than in a crisis situation. Your people will have no choice but to transition during a crisis when someone can't fulfill his or her leadership duties because of a death or a moral failure. You can't know when an emergency will happen, but you can plan for when it does.

Unfortunately, many churches and organizations don't have an emergency transition plan. Often this is because they don't like to think about their leader getting too sick to serve, dying, or making an unfortunate decision that disqualifies him or her from ministry. But the truth of the matter is that people get sick, everyone dies, and people do fail. Nothing would be harder on the people you would leave behind than your lack of preparation in those difficult circumstances. Think for a moment about how hard it would be for them to grieve your loss while at the same time scrambling to replace you! A transition in leadership is hard enough when it's planned; an unexpected transition with no plan in place is even harder to recover from. It's our duty as leaders to actively do whatever we can to help prepare our organizations for crisis-driven transitions.

Ross Parsley, who took over as interim pastor at New Life Fellowship in Colorado Springs after Ted Haggard's unfortunate moral scandal, also strongly believes in the importance of planning for crisis-driven transitions. He told me that his experience proved how critical it is to have a plan for every aspect of crisis management.[4] To do otherwise is simply an irresponsible choice for any church. You have to plan for the unexpected, so that you are ready and able to respond appropriately and help bring security to the church. This isn't something you should just figure out on the fly; it should be in writing so there is no confusion over how things will be orchestrated in the case of such an event.

Many years ago, we all recognized that Todd had the calling and ability to lead Christ Fellowship, so our board drafted an emergency transition plan to install him as our lead pastor if anything happened to me. Everyone was made aware that if for some reason I wasn't able to carry out my duties as senior pastor, he would be the one selected to serve in my place. We also passed a resolution that if anything ever happened to both Todd and me, leaving neither of us able to lead the church, our board would be assisted by a group of nationally recognized leaders (hand-picked by Todd, our board, and me) in selecting the next senior leader of Christ Fellowship. In the interim, members of our teaching team would take up the speaking responsibilities at our weekend services and the executive team in place would lead the day-to-day operations. Since the transition from my leadership to Todd's, the church has modified the crisis plan, but one is still in place. I'm sure that what we have created could be more detailed, but we are confident that it will assist us if we ever find ourselves in an unexpected situation.

TIPS FOR LEADING WELL IN CRISIS-DRIVEN TRANSITIONS

If you are transitioning into senior leadership, whether because of the illness, death, or moral failure of a predecessor, you need to have a plan for handling the emergency. Following is a list of tips I believe will help you lead well in crisis-driven transitions.

1. Be confident of your calling

In the case of Thomas Road Baptist Church, Jonathan got up and spoke to the congregation that first weekend, encouraging the church to remember and celebrate his father's life, and to keep pressing on toward what God had called them to. Then he met with the board and tasked them with the duty of determining the next steps for the church. He asked them to decide if they wanted to put together a search committee to find someone else. Only five weeks later the board met and voted to name Jonathan as the next pastor. He and the board took that decision to the church family to vote.

He remembers telling the church, "The role of the pastor is something that cannot be inherited, passed down, or left in a will. Rather, it's something God has to ordain and call you to."[5] He never wanted anyone to assume that he would automatically be the next pastor. There was little question of Jonathan's calling, since he had served for fourteen years as the executive pastor. But he still wanted to honor the vote of the staff and congregation to be sure that everyone believed it was in the church's best interest to have him as their new senior pastor.

Had Dr. Falwell spent some time in specific discussions with Jonathan, his staff, and his board about his eventual transition, a lot of the formalities taken before selecting and installing Jonathan could have been avoided. This also would have given Jonathan an opportunity to be more intentional in asking his dad to train him in some of the areas that he ended up feeling ill-equipped to take over. For example, one of the things Jonathan told me was that he didn't know a lot about shepherding people in a time of need—doing things like performing funerals or visiting parishioners in the hospital. His dad had managed to do it all when he was the senior pastor, so Jonathan wasn't well trained in how to do a lot of those things. He was made aware of the gravity of this when his dad's friend Owen Hawkins sent him a minister's guidebook to help him learn how to officiate over those congregational life changes.

While Jerry Jr.'s transition into his role as president of Liberty University was more expected, he also warns against a leader's moving forward with a transition if he's not called to do so. He said, "Make sure you are called to do what you are doing. It's not something you can try to force. That's the only reason it worked here for me. . . . Make sure you love it and enjoy what you are doing. I remember being a student, walking around looking at the campus and imagining how I wished it would look. I have had a long-term vision of what I wanted the university to become. My heart was in it for many years before I actually got into the role. I think that's key."[6]

Just like Jerry Falwell, Joel Osteen's father, John, didn't have a transition plan before his untimely death in the prime of his career as senior pastor of Lakewood Church. Joel's brother Paul remarked, "My dad was a planner. If he went on a mission trip he would tell us where the life insurance papers were and where his money was. When he was seventy-seven and got sick and was on dialysis because of renal failure it didn't take a rocket scientist to know he was in failing health. I would often ask, 'Dad, you planned everything in your life. Who is going to take over?' He'd reply, 'I didn't build the church. It's not my responsibility to continue the church.'"[7]

Unfortunately, this left the church leadership with little direction when he passed away. Joel was not sure of God's direction for him initially. He worked under his dad's leadership for seventeen years as the producer for Lakewood's televised sermons. His dad often encouraged him to preach, but he always declined, feeling more comfortable serving behind the scenes. But in early 1999, Joel felt compelled to preach his first sermon. He was unaware that it would be the last Sunday his father was alive. Suddenly he was needed in the pulpit. Joel continued preaching.[8]

Later that year, Joel Osteen was installed as senior pastor of Lakewood Church. Suddenly, thousands of people were relying on him for leadership. It was a tough adjustment for Joel, but over time, he and his siblings led their congregation through the loss of their founder to a place of great impact and influence in the kingdom of God.

Rob Hoskins of OneHope shared a story with me about a pivotal moment when he was confronted with an important question about whether he was truly called to his new role as president. His dad was critically ill with cancer and the ministry was going through a very difficult transition in leaving the Assemblies of God denomination to become independent. He had just left a meeting where he felt like a complete failure in his father's absence.

That evening he roomed with another guy who had also recently received the leadership baton from his father. He woke Rob up in the middle of the night and shared with him about his own sense of inadequacy and the challenges he had faced. Then he asked Rob, "Are you potted or are you planted? If you are potted, when the wind blows and trouble comes your way, you will move. But if you are planted, you won't move. You need to decide whether you are potted or planted in your ministry."

ARE YOU POTTED OR ARE YOU PLANTED?

Rob was convicted that night, so he purposed in his heart that he was going to plant himself in OneHope knowing this is where the Lord wanted him. He said, "It took that testing for me to have that certainty in my heart, especially because I'm a son. I had to question whether I was in this position only because he was my father. I had to get to the point where I knew I wasn't here because I'm Bob's son. I'm here because I am God's son, and he has appointed me for this time."[9]

Every leader needs the assurance that he is called to his position of leadership. And whether you are suddenly thrust into a leadership position due to a death or a moral failure, your congregation or the organization you serve will need you to be strong and confident in the calling God has given you. Put a stake in the ground and never look back! And on the hard days when the pressures and doubts mount, go back to your stake and remember God's calling and equipping. This will allow you to lead your people through their crisis and into the future.

2. Strengthen yourself in the Lord

There are going to be a lot of hard days ahead—emotionally, physically, and spiritually. Some days the only person you will have to stand by you is the Lord.

Remember the story in 1 Samuel 30 of David and his men at Ziklag? They returned from a campaign to find everything burned, their wives taken captive, and their goods stolen. The men turned their backs on David, threatening to stone him because they blamed him for their loss. I imagine the stress was high for David in that moment. He didn't have anyone to encourage him. His men had abandoned him, and he was left alone in his grief and despair.

When you find yourself in a leadership transition due to a crisis, you will sometimes feel alone—as though no one understands or can help you find your way. At times you may feel that the staff isn't supporting you, or your people don't believe in you. You may simply be grieving over your predecessor's passing or failure and finding no relief from your sadness. It's in those times that you must lean in to God and let Him be your strength.

The Bible tells us that when David was at his lowest point, alone and afraid, it was then that he found his strength in the Lord (v. 6). He ran to his Father in prayer for wisdom and guidance. After doing so, David rallied his men to pursue the enemy and get back what had been stolen. He turned their eyes from their loss to the mission to restore and bring freedom for the captives. And he was able to see God's hand at work in their loss.

When you constantly look to God for help and strengthen yourself in Him alone, He will help you endure the trials and press through to victory. Surround yourself with men and women of great faith who will encourage you along the way and lean in to God, your Father, who loves you and loves your people. He will help you.

3. Gather the right team of support around you

Churches and organizations struggle when they lose a leader for any reason. One of the things you can do to help bring health and vitality back to your organization after a loss or moral failure is to find someone—or, better yet, a team of people—to support you. They will help as you navigate the grief everyone is experiencing after the loss or removal of their leader. It's always an extremely emotional experience to make a transition after a death or moral crisis. Your people will be sad, or perhaps angry, and they will need emotional support. And frankly, you will probably need it as well.

When I asked Jonathan Falwell what his greatest challenge was initially after his dad's death, he said, "The greatest weight for me wasn't even ministry related. It was the fact that I lost my dad. It was a sudden situation. Dealing with that was my greatest struggle. Everything else was affected by the loss and grief I was going through."[10] Jonathan experienced the importance to the new leader of having a support team to hold up his arms and wipe his tears. You need someone who can stand by you and offer support as you embrace your new role and care for the heart of your people.

Right after we received news of Jerry Sr.'s death, John Maxwell and I flew up to spend an hour with Jonathan before we left the country for a speaking engagement. As we walked into Jerry and Macel's home, we found a weary Jonathan. As we talked with him, John and I both knew all he needed was the assurance of our presence and availability. We made sure he knew we loved his dad dearly and that we loved him and Jerry too. I took him by the shoulders, looked him in the eye, and said, "We are here for you, Jonathan." That's all he needed. That's all each of us needs in the face of crisis—someone to affirm and support us.

That person or team should also help give you insight and wisdom into the history and context of certain decisions. In the early days after Dr. Falwell's death, Jerry Jr. leaned heavily on some of his dad's friends and advisors. He said, "There were key individuals who privately advised me—people who had worked closely with Dad like Elmer Towns, Ron Godwin, and Mark Hine—and explained to me why things were done as they were at Liberty. They gave me the history about how certain things were handled and why they were set up as they were. I still obtain valuable advice from these people every day. I believe it was providential that these key men survived Dad. The transition would have been more difficult if they had not survived Dad and I had not had their wisdom and counsel available after Dad passed."[11]

When taking over as president of Walk Thru the Bible, my friend Phil Tuttle said, "I had to learn who to listen to. We had not established a mentoring environment in our organization, so seeking out wise counsel was the key to navigating that pivotal time in our organization."[12] These kinds of advisors will help you avoid pitfalls and be aware of any blind spots you may have in those early days after you take over leadership of your organization.

Surround yourself with people who love you, understand the challenges of ministry, and can provide context on the past and guidance for the future. They should be men and women of emotional and spiritual maturity who can stand by you and provide whatever support you need to move forward in your calling as the new leader for your church or organization on the next leg of the journey.

4. Keep pointing your people back to the mission

When people are uncertain, it will always bring a sense of calm and direction to those you are suddenly asked to lead if you can keep pointing them back to the mission of your organization.

Remind them frequently of God's commission to reach the world with the love and message of Christ.

This is of particular importance for any successor, but even more so when taking over in a crisis situation. People need the stability of what was right in the past. They also need reminders of what they are striving toward together in the future under your leadership. You need to help them understand that while you are a "new" leader, your agenda is built upon the foundation that has already been established.

Jonathan Falwell spoke about the importance of keeping people on mission during my interview with him. He explained,

> I had to remind our people that God's called us to go into all the world and make disciples of every nation. There has to be a recognition of that mission statement and the power of God. When God's man dies, His work never does. We need to understand we have to keep moving forward and realize we are human. . . . We need to recognize who God is; He is still on the throne. He has a purpose and plan, and will continue to provide. Whether we are in crisis or not, God has called us to this mission for today! The sign on the back wall of our church states: "Not I, but Christ." It's not about dad or me, but about Christ. Christ is still on the throne. We still have a mission to accomplish for His kingdom![13]

After a crisis due to a moral failure, it will be particularly difficult to help your people regain their focus on God's mission for your church or organization. In fact, in some cases, people can't refocus on the mission because they are too distracted by the scandal, and they end up leaving. Dan Southerland spoke about this very thing. He told me, "Our rally cry was, 'If you leave now, then you're committed to a man. If you stay now, you are committed to Jesus and His church.'"[14] This helped the congregations that he pastored to keep the right perspective.

Jason Meyer of Bethlehem Baptist Church talked at the Leadership Network Conference about helping people move through loss. He said, "During succession, we need to remind people to keep their eyes on the Lord, our one true Leader. Men will come and go, but His leadership will endure forever."[15]

> ONE MAN'S LOSS OR FAILURE
> DOESN'T CHANGE WHO GOD IS OR
> HIS PLAN FOR HIS CHURCH.

One man's loss or failure doesn't change who God is or His plan for His church. We need to remember this because people will constantly let us down. And, of course, everyone eventually dies. Now in the case of a moral failure of a senior leader, I know it can be absolutely devastating to the faith and growth development of your people. It's just a matter of fact: people entrust their spiritual growth to their leader, and when he betrays them, it legitimately rocks their foundations.

Your job as their new leader is to help them rebuild and shore up any cracks in their spiritual foundation. You need to help them see that the choices your predecessor made were his choices and not representative of the organization, of you as a leader, or of the message you are teaching. They need to be reminded that they must keep building their life on God's Word, which never changes based on circumstances or preferences. Dan Southerland coined a phrase that helps summarize this well: "The mess in the messenger does not change the message."[16]

As leaders, we have to help our people regain their focus on the message and mission of God's kingdom, and how He is uniquely moving at our church or organization. Then we have to help them focus outside themselves to stay mission-minded. This is critical because our enemy is real, and he will do anything he can to rob us of our focus. Betrayal, discouragement, doubt, anger, bitterness, and grief are all strategies our enemy uses to knock us off mission. Because of this, the banner of the mission of the church must be raised higher than ever before.

It's important to present an action plan that your people can execute in order to experience early victories after the crisis. It may be as simple as painting a widow's home, doing a food drive to help families that are out of work, fixing up a single mom's car, or taking a team to a local nursing home to bring joy to some very lonely and often-forgotten seniors. Get your people's focus back on serving others and sharing the love of God, and they will slowly but surely move past the sadness and back into their purpose.

And as your people execute your action plan to serve, celebrate every act of Christ's love. Celebrate answered prayer. Celebrate every life that has come to Christ. Celebration is so important in the healing and recovery process of a church going through a crisis. Mike Erre of First Evangelical Free Church in Fullerton, California, said, "Celebrate every little bit of what God is doing, even if it's not the whole thing. Find small things to celebrate before there are big, noticeable wins. The importance of celebration in crisis simply cannot be underestimated. You must determine what a win looked like before the crisis and adapt for what wins look like after the crisis."[17] Celebrating those wins helps your people get their eyes on the future.

I remember when Jerry Falwell Jr. stood at Liberty's graduation just a few short days after Jerry Sr.'s death. The first thing he did was confidently declare that all was well at Liberty University. His assurance that God was with them and would help them move forward gave the people some hope to hold on to in their grief and fear. Your people need to see that God has not lifted His hand away from you. In fact, it's just the opposite. He is closer than ever in crisis because the more desperate the situation, the greater His work.

5. Make changes slowly

After the death or moral failure of your predecessor, do not make change your first order of business. The loss or removal of your predecessor is change enough for the people you are now leading. Your first priority in this type of crisis situation is to love them through their grief and help them see God's presence and care. Change will come in time, but you have to be very careful about the timing, motives, and value of the change. Tread lightly through the prospect of change, knowing it will be far better for you to take your time and work on healing and strengthening your people first. Once your people have experienced some time and distance from their grief or disappointment, and they have gotten to know you and your heart for them, they will be more receptive to the changes that you feel are necessary to the growth and edification of the organization.

Whenever you do introduce proposed changes, always help your people understand that the reason for the change is directly tied to their heritage and in line with Scripture, their sure foundation in rocky times. And do whatever you can to engage people in a number of discussions so you can alleviate any concerns or questions about the coming changes.

When I interviewed Dan Southerland, he relayed a story from when he first took over at Potential Church (formerly named Flamingo Road Church) in Cooper City, Florida. This was after the former leader had experienced a moral failure. An associate from another local church asked Dan what changes he thought were needed at Flamingo Road Church. For about thirty minutes, Dan rattled off a long list. The man then very kindly said to Dan, "The greatest advice I can give you is love them and teach them for two years before you change anything. You're going in with no credit. The guy before you has destroyed all trust in the pastoral office, all trust in authority, and all trust in leadership. You have to build trust."[18] So Dan spent two years at Flamingo loving the people, teaching the Word, and getting the church on the same page, before he changed anything.

Looking back, Dan is so glad his friend admonished him to move slowly through change and to focus his attention on meeting the people's basic needs for restoration after experiencing such betrayal. I asked Dan if he could summarize this tip for others who become successors after a moral failure. He said, "Go slow. . . . Don't major on change. They have already had the most traumatic change they can have. Their ability to handle change is used up until you reestablish trust."[19]

If I could give you any advice about change in the midst of a crisis, it would be to avoid it when possible. Take your time and be prayerful. Consult your board and your key advisors before moving forward with any changes that may jeopardize your people's security or support.

6. Rebuild trust

An important crisis transition tip, particularly in a moral failure, is to remember that it is going to take time to rebuild the trust of the people in you as a leader and in your church or organization. Lance Witt said, "People will automatically ask, 'If we trusted the last guy and he let us down, what should make us trust it won't happen with you?'"[20] I would say this is a valid question in this situation. After all, trust is a leader's currency, and when that trust is broken, it's hard to regain.

> TRUST IS A LEADER'S CURRENCY,
> AND WHEN THAT TRUST IS BROKEN,
> IT'S HARD TO REGAIN.

In his book *Messy Church*, Ross Parsley said, "Trust is really all that a church has. . . . Churches aren't supposed to be about selling God stuff or producing Christian products for the masses to consume. The church that Jesus is building is a family of relationships where the only currency is the good word of the leaders, as well as the people's trust. Integrity is the bedrock upon which the church is led, encouraged, and challenged by our leaders. This trust is the platform from which we serve."[21]

As Lance said, "It takes years to build trust, but seconds to betray."[22] And trust and love are not the same thing. Jason Bolin learned that everyone was skeptical that he would be trustworthy, since they had trusted his dad, who had let them down. Jason said, "I confused love and trust. They are not the same thing."[23] He knew the people loved him, but it took him some time to realize they didn't yet trust him. He said, "What they gave me was their love, not their trust. Trust had to be earned."[24]

One of the ways you can rebuild trust is through honesty and communication. Ross Parsley suggested that you tell the people details the best you can. "When you don't know, say, 'I don't know what's going on in regards to this situation yet.' That is better than making something up. I think people get in trouble in a crisis situation when they put on appearances they can't keep up. . . . I was truly transparent. It worked in my favor not to be polished and just to share the best I could."[25]

Dan Southerland, who has taken over two churches after the former leader had a moral failure, spoke with me about how important transparency was for a congregation to learn how to move forward and trust again. Explaining what he shared with the congregation, he said,

I'd tell them that we work in the sunshine. Then I'd tell them, "We won't celebrate the details of the failure, but you need to know that this was an affair, he's disqualified as a leader over this congregation, nobody else has had an affair on the team, and nobody else is disqualified." . . . I grew up in a church where they swept these kinds of issues under the carpet, and our congregation never recovered. Transparency is the key to leading in times like this. . . . The church has to know what is reasonable to share. Not knowing is worse than knowing.[26]

However, keep in mind that you and your church or organization will fall under a lot of scrutiny in those early days after a crisis. Every bit of communication you dispense needs to be thoughtfully censored as Dan suggested, but it also needs to be carefully crafted for clarity, thus minimizing the chance of misunderstanding. Ross Parsley said, "Every e-mail is a press release in a crisis."[27] Boy, if that isn't the truth! The broader the impact of the moral failure, the more significant this fact is. Every statement and decision you make is magnified and more easily misconstrued in an environment where people are trying to collect themselves after a crisis. Think critically about how your words and actions will be received by those who hear and see them. Consult with your core team of leaders or an outside consultant, if needed, to help you gauge the impact of the messages you are sending in these situations.

《《 Every e-mail is a press release in a crisis. 》》
−ROSS PARSLEY

Along with sharing the details necessary for disclosure that will lead to healing, I think it's also important to communicate what steps the leadership is taking to help rehabilitate and restore the fallen leader. The congregation will be mourning the failure for a number of reasons, but one of the primary reasons will be because they loved their pastor, and they are saddened by his sin. You will rebuild trust, particularly in the new and remaining leadership, when you demonstrate godly compassion and grace for their former leader.

In addition to being transparent in communicating with the congregation, you will need to prepare yourself to communicate well with the staff as well. Dan said, "The church healed up much faster than the staff and core leaders. The closer you work with the person who violated your trust, the longer it will take you to get over it."[28] Dan indicated to me that it took, on average, two to three years for the team to fully recover and be able to minister from a healthy, open place. When I asked him what he believed were the most effective means of influence for the incoming leader, he said an investment of time, patience, and a lot of love was essential to reestablishing trust with them.

7. Create accountability with transparency

It's extremely important in a crisis situation resulting from a moral failure to immediately gather an inner circle of people who can hold you accountable as you take over leadership. Your people need to know you will make the right choices; therefore, you will need the accountability to hold you to a standard of excellence that your predecessor might have neglected.

So many churches end up closing their doors or experiencing hurtful splits after a moral failure from their leader, because the trust in leadership has been broken so severely. The people simply can't rebound and trust again. So after you select an inner circle, immediately share who they are with your people, so that they know you are being intentional about keeping this from happening again. I believe people will more readily submit to your authority when they know you are submitted to authority. It sets a precedent and builds trust that had been previously violated.

There is no greater time for the enemy to snag us up than when we are isolated from others. When we don't have anyone providing a spiritual covering against temptation and sinfulness, it is far easier to stumble. But when we have someone there who can pray with us and head us off before we make poor choices that could hurt our walk with the Lord and the people we serve, we naturally build a safety net of protection.

Leadership in ministry can be a lonely place. When you are leading and shepherding others in their walk, you are expected to function as though you have it all together. It can feel as if there is very little room for you to be your true self. And you may feel pressure to be perfect and flawless. Let me remind you that you aren't perfect—you are simply expected to strive for righteousness through the power of the Holy Spirit alive in you.

Remember, though, that we are all tempted by sin! Sometimes I think as pastors leading others, we subconsciously exempt ourselves from this reality. We think because we are studying and delivering God's Word, and are surrounded by God's people doing God's work, that Satan can't tempt us to step outside the parameters of obedience and piety. Hello? Anyone who thinks that is the perfect candidate for destruction, since the agenda of the enemy is to destroy the work and impact of the kingdom. Who better to start with, than the leaders of God's church, who should be serving as the very examples of holiness?

The first plot of the enemy is to make you believe you can stand up under temptation by yourself. He wants you to believe that if you are busying yourself with God's work, you won't be tempted. Second, when you find yourself tempted to step outside the boundaries of God's protective Word, the enemy will try to make you believe you can fight it alone. Or third, if you do give in, he'll tell you that you can hide it or minimize its effects.

Satan wants you to believe you are alone, because when you are alone, you'll be tempted to believe that no one will find out about your wrong choice. You'll also be tempted to believe you can "manage" your sin and not let it snowball into something destructive—both to yourself and your ministry. Don't believe those lies.

Temptation is a very dangerous place to walk alone, friend. I truly believe the best way you can steer clear of acting on those struggles is by running to a trusted inner circle of people who see you as the human that you are. Ask them to pray with you and help you make decisions that will protect yourself and your ministry.

I think a lot of leaders in ministry avoid getting close to anyone for transparent accountability because they fear that being vulnerable with someone else about their struggles will open them up to judgment. But the solution is not to avoid accountability. Instead, find someone who knows you and loves you for who you are. Find someone whose agenda is to listen, pray, guide, and guard. Who will provide a safe place for you to be honest. Who desires to lovingly stand by you and firmly undergird you in truth and obedience. And most important, find someone who has experienced wisdom and credible accountability.

My friend Chris Hodges, the senior pastor at Church of the Highlands in Alabama, was intentional about selecting five men as his overseers, and I was one of them. He has tasked us with the responsibility of providing leadership and oversight for the church, and in the selection of his successor should he ever have a moral failure. He wants his people to know that he holds himself accountable to these men and will submit himself to their leadership and judgment if needed. He even went so far as to include this stipulation in the by-laws of the church so there was no confusion or question about what should take place in that type of situation. I believe this plan brings an incredible amount of security to his congregation, so imagine how much it would comfort a congregation devastated by a leader's moral failure.

Regardless of how you took over the leadership of your church or organization, you need to have your own accountability team and covenant. Larry Stockstill recommends that these accountability partners be over sixty and successful in their own leadership and in their own fight for integrity. He adds that it is valuable after a crisis to introduce these men to your staff and congregation and say, "If you have any problems with me as pastor, I want you to feel free to contact these men, because I am accountable to them."[29]

The need for accountability and oversight *before* an incident of moral indiscretion is magnified *after* a moral failure and dismissal.

Ross Parsley recognized this need immediately at New Life. He said, "New Life needed a steady and consistent hand at the plow in the aftermath of the loss of a beloved pastor. Our church needed an extended family that would provide love, wisdom, experience and resources. We found that in Gateway Church through Pastor Robert Morris."[30]

Ross also said that in order to get credibility back, they needed to borrow someone else's. That, he felt, was also the role of the overseers that God brought to New Life during that season. That way, the church family came to trust there wasn't widespread corruption, and they could begin rebuilding.

One of the things Ross suggested is that you build your inner circle of overseers well before they would be needed. Then expose your people to them frequently, so there is a familiarity and relational equity available in times of crisis. He made the valid point that when crafting a plan for managing crisis, the accountability and oversight team can't just be in the pastor's pocket or exist on paper alone. Your staff and your church family must know them, and they must be a part of your extended church family. This helps bring even more credibility to the process for managing a moral failure, and it helps the staff feel more secure knowing how the powers will be divided should an issue come up.

Along with creating an accountability team of individuals who would hold him accountable to certain standards, Dan Southerland made adjustments to the way he interacted with staff, being especially open by giving them more access to his heart. He also started making decisions as a team, so there was little opportunity for him to find himself alone. He said,

I set up accountability for me both times. I was very open. I also became very close with staff. As a result of the failure in their prior leaders, we moved away from a uni-pastor model where the pastor was in charge of everything, to a board and elder-driven model. We needed to reestablish trust, and I believe this model is simply biblical. That helped immensely because people started thinking, "Not only can we trust this new guy but this new guy is not the only guy making the decisions anymore." To mark this decision, we changed the by-laws to say we were now going to share leadership. I am the visionary and the main teacher, but we make our decisions as a team.[31]

8. Travel the high road

It may prove challenging to speak well of a leader who failed morally, particularly right after the news comes out and everyone is talking about it. And seeing the pain that people are experiencing as a result of the former pastor's dismissal can just break your heart, making it challenging to uplift that leader's name. However, you still need to take the high road.

It can be similarly difficult after the death of a leader who left certain things undone, or who didn't do the things he needed to do to keep the church in a healthy position when he was alive. You can't undo the past, but you can certainly do your best to redirect negative conversations to the great things the individual did put in motion and the years he committed himself to the ministry among them. People won't always agree, and they may have trouble leaving the past in the past. I assure you that these are valid, human feelings. However, you need to remember that you set the example for how this person will be spoken about and remembered in the future. His poor choices will no doubt affect his legacy negatively, but you shouldn't add to it.

Just as David exhibited mercy, grace, and generosity to those who didn't make it all the way when he shared the spoils of victory at Ziklag, we need to extend extra mercy, grace, and generosity to a fallen leader. Take the high road and love the sinner, not the sin.

My grandfather used to tell me, "Son, always do the most loving thing." He encouraged me to believe the best of others, to speak the best about them, and to give my best to them, whether that be in protecting their reputation or restoring dignity where possible.

> ALWAYS DO THE MOST LOVING THING.

———

A crisis-driven transition is the hardest kind of transition; and the fundamentals of leadership are never more needed than when you lead through crises. Focus on your higher purpose as a church or organization. In fact, I would suggest you make that the theme of your first sermon series when you take over leadership. It will bring clarity and direction to your people and overshadow the heartache they are feeling.

You will need to be very intentional about showing love and grace to your people, remembering that everyone will grieve in different stages at different times. Be patient and make yourself available to love them wherever they are on the journey to healing.

Never underestimate the importance of being transparent at all times, in all things. Build accountability around you and the organization from respected leaders outside of your church's four walls. And consider seeking out counsel from others who have walked a similar road. Draw your inner circle of leaders to your side as you get adjusted, leaning on them to help you make decisions for the overall direction and management of the organization. Call them to a time of prayer and fasting to seek the wisdom and blessing of God.

> MAKE EVERY EFFORT TO CELEBRATE
> SMALL AND LARGE VICTORIES
> AS THEY TAKE PLACE.

Make every effort to celebrate small and large victories as they take place. This will bring joy and hope to your people as they see that God is still working among them. And use common sense; don't make any major decisions or changes right away. Focus on stabilizing your organization and the healing of your people through your presence and confidence. This is your most important role after the death or moral failure of your predecessor. Your people need to regain trust, and that will only happen through the example of your leadership in the midst of their crisis.

Above everything you do, lean in to God to help you do your very best to bring healing and love to the people you serve. Remember, God does His best work in us through times of crisis. Paul reminded us in 1 Corinthians 10:13 that there is no test or trial that you could face that isn't common to man. What you are facing can be used to lead others through their own trials. I know God will lead you through the storm, and you will not only survive, but thrive. Press on in strength and lead your people through their pain well.

As Dan Southerland put it, "We are in the recovery business. We are in the reconciliation business. We shouldn't be afraid of churches that have been wounded so deeply. If we go slowly and love deeply, and trust God, the greatest days of the church are ahead."[32]

FINISHING STRONG

Creating a Legacy

> What you leave behind is not what is engraved in stone
> monuments, but what is woven into the lives of others.
>
> —PERICLES[1]

When Henrietta Mears was a child, doctors told her mother that she would be blind by the age of thirty. But as a young adult, Mears became convinced of God's purpose for her life. So she read and studied all she could in case her eyesight failed. Later, against the advice of her physicians, she enrolled in classes at the University of Minnesota, where she ended up graduating with honors.

At first, Mears taught high school chemistry. But then she was asked to serve as the director of Christian education at the First Presbyterian Church in Hollywood. There she wrote her own Sunday school curriculum and started Gospel Light Publications, which is still one of the leaders in Christian publications today. She also bought a retreat center in the San Bernardino Mountains so she could further educate and disciple young people through a daily Bible study.

Henrietta never wavered in fulfilling her God-given destiny during her generation. "When I consider my ministry, I think of the world. Anything less than that would not be worthy of Christ, nor of his will for my life."[2] Three years after her arrival at the church, Sunday school attendance grew from four hundred to four thousand. And during her tenure, more than four hundred young people entered full-time Christian service.

One of the young people who was greatly impacted by Henrietta Mears's ministry was Dr. Bill Bright. Dr. Bright accepted Christ in Mears's retreat home Bible study at the age of twenty-four. He went on to attend Fuller Theological Seminary in preparation for full-time ministry.

While there, Bright was up late studying for a Greek exam one night, when he felt strongly impressed that God wanted him to give his life to evangelizing the world. He sensed that he was to start by ministering to college students. So he and his wife, Vonette, obediently yielded their lives to full-time ministry in 1951. They founded Campus Crusade for Christ, which later became known as CRU, to win campuses to Christ. And the rest, as they say, is history!

CRU has grown to be the largest Christian ministry in the world, and Dr. Bright had tremendous impact through the fifty-two years that he oversaw the ministry. To this day, CRU has a ministry presence in 191 countries around the world. Bill Bright's booklet *The Four Spiritual Laws*, has been translated into more than two hundred languages, and more than 2.5 billion copies have been distributed worldwide. His film *Jesus*, about the life and sacrifice of Christ, is the most translated motion picture in history, with more than 974 languages accounted for. Roughly 5.5 billion people have viewed it since its release in 1979, and 201.6 million people have made decisions for Christ after seeing it.[3]

Dr. Bright's impact in the Christian world is undeniable. I was privileged to know him personally and serve on his board for Global Pastors Network, an initiative to train and equip pastors around the world. When he knew the time of his death was nearing, he called a gathering of the board members and directors where he literally passed out batons to each of us, charging us to continue carrying out our mission to fulfill the Great Commission. A few months later John Maxwell and I visited him in his home just weeks before he died. During that visit he grasped our hands and pleaded with us, through labored breath, to carry the baton faithfully to the end. Today, I still have the baton he gave me sitting in my office to remind me of the testimony of his great leadership and his challenge to me. And it represents the legacy he left us all.

I can honestly say he was one of the most prolific men of faith I have ever had the privilege of knowing. His faith and passion for the Word never faded; it only grew with intensity as he neared the end of his life. And to think, he might never have had the impact for Christ that he did, had it not been for Henrietta Mears. Her passion and commitment to educate and train the next generation of Christian leaders led her to share the gospel with him as a young man and help him grow in his faith so he could literally reach the world for Christ.

It's a known fact that Henrietta accomplished many amazing,

long-standing things for the kingdom of God in her generation. However, I'm confident that if we could talk to her today, she would say that her greatest impact rests in those who accepted Christ as a result of her ministry and then went on to impact the world for the Lord after she was gone. Dr. Bill Bright is a legacy of Mears's ministry.

Mordecai Ham was another influential Christian leader in his time. Born on April 2, 1877, in a small Kentucky town, he resisted God's call to ministry because he had grown up seeing his father and grandfather, both ministers themselves, living in poverty. His ambition and desire for a more successful life for himself and his family drove him to pursue business instead. However, six months after marrying his first wife, Bessie, he could no longer resist God's plans for him to spread the gospel, so he left his career as a salesman to enter the ministry full-time.

He traveled the country preaching the saving power of Jesus Christ at revivals and warning against societal sins such as alcoholism. In his thirty years of ministry, he led more than three hundred thousand people to faith. Perhaps the most notable of those he led to Christ is the best-known man of faith in the twentieth century, Dr. Billy Graham, who himself has led hundreds of thousands of people to faith in Christ through his evangelistic crusades.

Graham easily recalls the day he heard Mordecai Ham share the gospel. Just a few days shy of his sixteenth birthday, he joined a friend at church in Charlotte, North Carolina, for an evangelistic revival with five thousand other people. Thinking religion was for sissies, Graham didn't expect much, but Mordecai Ham spoke with such conviction and authority that young Billy thought he was speaking directly to him when he pronounced that all were sinners. Fearing Ham's message, Graham went home and wrestled all night long with what Ham had shared. The next day, he returned to the revival tent and heard another message of conviction for sin, and the love of God. Graham went forward during the invitation that day and gave his heart to Christ, dedicating his life to God's service.[4]

Today Billy Graham is one of the most admired men in the world. He has preached the gospel to more people in live audiences than anyone else in history—nearly 215 million people in more than 185 countries and territories. Hundreds of millions more have been reached through television, video, film, and webcasts. And he has led hundreds of thousands of people to make personal decisions for Christ.[5] He's also highly sought after by United States presidents and dignitaries, for spiritual advice and counsel.

Donna, and I had the privilege of meeting him in his home in the mountains of North Carolina a few years ago. As we sat there talking over root beer floats, I kept asking him to share stories and memories from his years of ministry, but he rarely obliged. He just kept redirecting the conversation back to our ministry with Christ Fellowship because he wanted to focus on the future work of the Lord. He constantly validated and affirmed what we were doing and planning because Dr. Graham has a humble and eternal perspective of the Great Commission. Our conversation with him reminded me again that God is—and will be—at work to complete His plan in and through willing vessels. Great leaders like Dr. Graham don't try to hold on to the victories of the past. They pass the baton into reliable hands and cheer and celebrate the new victories for the kingdom of God.

I believe Dr. Bill Bright is the Paul of our generation, and Dr. Billy Graham, the Peter. Henrietta Mears and Mordecai Ham had no idea how they would be touching the world when they led these two amazing giants of the faith to Christ. Neither knew the impact they would have through their faithful service to our Lord. Neither ever could have imagined the people who would come to know Christ simply because they obediently fulfilled their calling. Their legacies are far richer than I believe they ever could have dreamed because they left a heritage of faith for others to follow.

LEAVING LASTING LEGACIES

Sometimes, as leaders, we tend to focus so much on the immediate demands of our organizations that we don't give much thought to our legacy. If we had the chance to speak with Henrietta Mears or Mordecai Ham, I highly doubt either of them would say they gave much thought to how their investment in Bill Bright or Billy Graham would affect generations to come. They were simply faithful to the calling God had on their lives. But I'm confident they did know they were ministering to some very special men of God as each stepped into dynamic roles for the kingdom.

We have to get in the habit of pulling back to assess how our daily choices impact the future. Everything we do today lays a foundation for tomorrow. And we want to build a solid foundation for our ministry to stand long after we are gone. In his book *The 21 Irrefutable Laws of Leadership*, John Maxwell wrote, "Achievement comes to someone when he is able to do great things for himself. Success comes when he empowers his followers to do great things with him. Significance comes when he develops leaders to do great things for him. But a legacy is created only when a person puts his organization into the position to do great things without him."[6]

> EVERYTHING WE DO TODAY LAYS A FOUNDATION FOR TOMORROW.

What truth! I am convinced that there is truly no greater joy and fulfillment in life than to leave a legacy of faith for those behind you.

I'm a big believer in generational blessing, because I have been a recipient of the blessing of those who have faithfully carried the baton before me. So for me, it is a tremendous blessing to be able to witness the beginning of a new era at Christ Fellowship under Todd's leadership. He has taken up the next leg of ministry that my great-grandfather started in the 1890s and passed on to my grandfather, who then passed it on to me. And I assure you, there is little else as gratifying as knowing that while I contributed to the kingdom in my day, I now get to witness the amazing job my son is doing to impact the world with the love and message of Jesus Christ in his generation.

My prayer of legacy is that my life will be an encouragement, not only to my own son, but to other leaders as well. I want to encourage them to run well and run hard to the very end. I am committed to running until my Savior calls me home because the heritage of faithful service that has been passed down to me is too precious to set aside for anything else.

I often sit in my office and study the photos of men who have profoundly impacted me by leaving me a legacy in which I share. The first is a picture of my great-grandfather who was a circuit-riding preacher in the 1800s. Beneath his photo is a picture of my grandfather preaching behind the pulpit in which I preached my first sermon at age sixteen. Below his photo you'll find photos of Reverend Billy Graham and Dr. Bill Bright, both great mentors and friends. And finally, there is a picture of Reverend Books Linn, a godly man who believed in me as a young man and brought Donna and me to Florida so I could serve as a youth pastor at Church in the Gardens in Palm Beach Gardens during the summer of 1968. Through Reverend Linn, we met the precious people with whom God would partner us to birth Christ Fellowship in our home.

The photos of these men in a quiet corner of my office remind me of how rich a heritage I have received through them. Each one played an important role in forming me as a leader who is passionate for the things of God. Each inspired me to rise up and fulfill my calling in my generation. Each was a heritage builder who taught me valuable lessons about the importance of transitions in life. They taught me to sow into future generations so the ministry of the Lord never ceases to have far-reaching impact.

I realize so vividly at this stage in my life and ministry how vital it is to raise up and inspire spiritual sons for the kingdom work. I know this practice deepens my legacy in the imprints I will leave behind, so I've invested myself in that practice during the days of influence that I still have. In fact, I experience no greater joy than when I engage, equip, and empower emerging leaders to run their race well.

> I'M A BIG BELIEVER IN GENERATIONAL BLESSING.

As John Maxwell indicated, legacy is crafted when we move from success to significance. How well we make the transition from one to the other is the true witness of our leadership. And that significance is forged only as we empower others to lead from their position of strength and influence in their generation. We have to make room for others to lead. We have to come up with a plan to hand off the baton so the next runner can make strides in his leg of the race.

I am so blessed to have had this modeled for me at an early age. My grandfather is such a great example of leading through transition, because he was always eager to share ministry with us younger guys. As a young man, I tried to understand why Grandpa passed the baton when he did. He was still strong at the time. Yet, he did what was best for the work of God, and became the number one supporter of his successor. I am forever grateful for the legacy my grandpa passed down to me. My prayer is that I will be an inspiration to others as he was to me.

I recently traveled to Zimbabwe to do leadership training for several thousand pastors and Christian leaders from all over Africa. As I was preparing to share my first of several lessons with them that week, I stood in the wings of the stage and watched a video that had been prepared to introduce me and the ministry at Christ Fellowship. I couldn't help but get sentimental as I reviewed all the Lord has allowed us to be a part of through the years.

My heart was so full of gratitude and my eyes were brimming with tears because in that moment I was so acutely aware of the legacy my grandfather had left me. Everything our Christ Fellowship family has experienced over the years was started in his heart and through his ministry. I could never have been so privileged to stand on that stage that day had it not been for the incredible impact he had on my life as young boy.

He taught me how to be a leader through his steady affirmation, encouragement, and empowerment. He never went to a school of leadership or had any formal leadership training. He simply modeled leadership in all he did so I learned and grew in my own leadership by observing his consistent godliness in both his private and public life.

Last year I was invited to speak at a church convention in Ohio that my grandfather had started more than sixty years ago. All weekend long I ran into people he had touched. They shared story after story with me about how he had impacted them for eternity, through the lessons they learned from him or the way they saw he lived his life. He loved people just as they were, always striving to be an extension of our loving Father God. It was greatly reinforced to me through those conversations just how powerful his life of faithful service had been. I don't think we realized that we had a giant among us.

And I don't believe he ever had any indications that his legacy of ministry would have the global impact it has today. He never got to see just how his faithfulness to the Lord would produce such a harvest of fruit in the kingdom. But I truly believe he sees glimpses from his window in heaven. The joy of legacy has to be one of his greatest crowns today. I cannot wait to be reunited with him one day so I can tell him all the stories of life change and transformation I have witnessed because of the legacy of faith and leadership he left me. Everything Christ Fellowship has been blessed to be a part of over the years is a direct result of the legacy he left us.

> THAT'S WHAT LEADERSHIP TRANSITIONS ARE REALLY ALL ABOUT—POURING INTO OTHERS SO THEY CAN RISE UP TO THEIR CALLING.

That's what leadership transitions are really all about—pouring into others so they can rise up to their calling to impact the world with the love and message of Jesus Christ. My grandfather was a strong, godly leader, resolute in his unwavering faith. I could look up to him for wisdom and affirmation, knowing he would do whatever possible to help me be all that God had called me to be. That's a true legacy. That's what we all need to strive for in our leadership transitions. We need to pass on the baton of faith and help others run their best race.

And we need to strive to do our very best to plan and prepare for inevitable and unexpected transitions. I hope that by now you are as convinced as I am about how important it is for your church to have a transition plan, so that the next generation of leaders can step up into their calling at the appropriate time. And equally, I hope you understand how important it is for your church or organization to prepare by putting resolutions in place to manage transitions born out of crisis. You simply cannot afford to neglect the proper planning for those kinds of transitions, because too much is at stake. And frankly, you don't want your legacy to be marred by your lack of planning for uncertainties. Show others in your ministry how important transition is by planning for it and executing your plan the best you can.

After thirty years of ministry at Christ Fellowship, I'm more excited about the coming years than ever. Since I passed the baton of leadership to Todd, God has truly honored our transition. The explosive growth in the last couple of years has forced us to go from four services a weekend to six. We recently opened new ministry centers in the Boynton Beach Mall, in New York City, and in Okeechobee, Florida, and are currently in the process of developing our ministry center in Stuart, Florida. When I look back, I can't help but recognize that our ministry in the early days was simply laying the foundation for all God is doing among us today and will continue to do in the future.

I'm also so humbled that after I passed on the baton to Todd, God had another baton for me to pick up and run with to lead EQUIP. I am enjoying traveling the world to work with the most influential Christian leaders on each continent. And by the way, I'm already thinking about and planning for my next transition. I have even begun recruiting my successor. When the time comes to pass that baton, I'll be excited to see what God has in store for the next leg of global ministry. And who knows? God may even have another race for me to run or a special spot for me where I can cheer the other runners on to the finish line. Regardless of what's next, I want to keep the faith and fight the good fight so I can finish the race He has for me (2 Tim. 4:7).

What about you? Have you given thought to your spiritual legacy? What do you want to leave behind for those who will follow you? What kind of kingdom impact do you want to have on future generations? I believe God allows us the opportunity to be a part of crafting an impactful legacy when we have the right perspective about transitions. When our focus is less on ourselves and more on what's best for our successor and our organization, we lay the groundwork for our leadership legacy.

Though you were created for eternity, your leadership privileges are only for a season. You have to be ready to hand off the baton when the timing is right. I really believe that your legacy depends on you having an expectant, willing heart toward the transition process. When you are open to constructive conversations about making room for someone else to step in, God will guide you to the right timing and the right person, for His glory.

> TRANSITION REALLY COMES
> DOWN TO BEING AN ISSUE OF
> HUMILITY AND SURRENDER.

Transition really comes down to being an issue of humility and surrender, if you think about it. All the practical things we've discussed in this book have hopefully been helpful to you as you plan with intentionality and troubleshoot inevitable issues along the way to your own transition in leadership. But the most important thing to consider is the fact that God's work is for God's sake—not our own. What we get to be a part of in ministry is not about us! It's not about making our names famous—it's about making His name famous. It's not about what we build or lead—it's about what God chooses to do in and through us by the power of His Spirit at work in our hearts and through our lives. Everything we are a part of is for His glory. When that is your realization, it forces you to a place of humility and surrender in the transition process because He alone is the priority, and His plans for His church are what matters above anything else.

When we surrender ourselves to His lordship over our lives, we are essentially signing away our rights to what we may want or think we need. Don't get me wrong here. He delights in fulfilling our deepest longings. His loving-kindness knows no limits. But ultimately, He is sovereign, and He has a plan to execute. We get to be a small part of that plan, and it's our job to stay chained to the stake we put in the ground when we surrendered ourselves to a life of service to Him.

> TRANSITION IS NOT ONLY THE
> GREATEST TEST OF YOUR
> LEADERSHIP; IT IS YOUR LEGACY.

Your legacy is fulfilled when you humbly and obediently hand off the baton when it's your time to do so. When God asks you to step away or to step into something new, be ready; because when you do so with grace and humility, fully surrendered to His call, you leave a legacy worth following.

Transition is not only the greatest test of your leadership; it is your legacy. Transition well.

AFTERWORD

By Todd Mullins

When I look back at our transition, it's easy for me to see how my dad prioritized and demonstrated its importance for our church. Great leaders like my dad see the change that needs to happen and are constantly preparing themselves and their people for that change. It takes vision to look down the road and help others grow in their leadership capacity so they are ready when the time comes. These great leaders constantly model, mentor, motivate, and steadily give their job away so they can take on the next challenge God has for them.

My dad defines this kind of great leader. From the beginning, he coached me up to help me reach my potential and realize my calling. Long before our transition took place, he made room for me to lead. He didn't use up all the "leadership oxygen" in our organization. A lot of leaders try to hold on to as much leadership responsibility as possible, either because they think that is their "job" or because they believe no one can do it as well as they can. My dad did the opposite. He understood that his job was to raise up leaders who could lead large areas of ministry because he was focused on the long-term health and strength of the organization. And he knew this would require more than one great man's effort. I believe that this, coupled with his consistent verbal affirmation of me in front of others, set the stage for a healthy transition.

As I said, great leaders don't hold on to power, but it certainly isn't easy to give it away. Years ago, I heard a senior pastor say that the hardest part of ministry wasn't planting a church, or building the ministry—it was giving away what he had built to the next generation. I have never forgotten that insight. As my father and I began our season of transition, I knew that *this senior leadership responsibility wasn't mine to take; it was his to give.* That truth challenged me to stay ready to lead, without trying to grasp at something before its due time. I had to trust that my dad—and my spiritual authority—would know that right time.

My father was quite young when he transferred leadership to me and my wife, Julie. He could have had many more great years ahead of him in that lead position, yet he chose to pass the baton so we could run the race God had set before us. He wanted to give me enough of an opportunity to lead from the senior position and keep the church young and moving forward. We all look back and agree that we transitioned at just the perfect time because he had led the church to a great place of strength and momentum.

It meant a lot to me that my dad had the wisdom and humility to make the handoff when he did. He always had everyone's best interest in mind. And he still does today. He hasn't gone any-where. Yes, he has taken on some new endeavors as the Lord has opened the doors, but he is still very much a part of our team. And as we made the transition, he has become our biggest "cheer-leader"—vocally affirming where the church is heading and the new approaches to ministry we have taken.

The church looks different today than it did under my father's leadership, but it has the same values, the same heart, and the same mission as we had in those early years. The greatest thing my parents transferred to us wasn't the leadership responsibil-ity—it was their love for the local church. Their commitment and dedication to building church was not only contagious, but it laid the foundation for all we are getting to do today! We believe 1 Corinthians 2:9 tells us "the BEST is yet to come!"

And I believe the best is yet to come for you too. Let's be faith-ful, in our generation, to plan for our own transitions so that God can continue to work in and through the generations yet to come.

NOTES

Chapter 1

1. Edythe Draper, *Draper's Book of Quotations for the Christian World* (Wheaton: Tyndale, 1992), 10740.
2. Sam Borden, "For U.S. Relayers, Dread of Another Dropped Baton," *New York Times*, July 23, 2012, http://www.nytimes.com/2012/07/23 /sports/olympics/olympics-2012-us-track-relays-hope-to-avoid-another -baton-drop.html?_r=0.
3. Ibid.
4. "Hour of Power pastor Robert Schuller retiring." *The Star* (Toronto), July 11, 2010, http://www.thestar.com/life/2010/07/11/hour_of_ power_pastor_robert_schuller_retiring.html.
5. Associated Press, "'Hour of Power' Preacher Removed by Father," Fox News, October 26, 2008, http://www.foxnews.com/story/2008/10/26 /hour-power-preacher-removed-by-father/.
6. Gillian Flaccus, "Crystal Cathedral founder's daughter aims to lead, heal," *USA Today*, June 25, 2009, http://usatoday30.usatoday.com /news/religion/2009-06-25-crystal-cathedral_N.htm.
7. John Elizondo, "Three Killeen pastors die in rollover crash," October 11, 2013, http://www.kxxv.com/story/23665521/three-killeen-pastors -die-in-fatal-rollover-crash.

Chapter 2

1. William Bridges, *Managing Transitions: Making the Most of Change* (Philadelphia: Da Capo, 2009), 23.
2. Bob Russell and Bryan Bucher, *Transition Plan* (Louisville: Minister's Label: 2010), 45.
3. For more information on the five levels of leadership, see Mark Martin, "John Maxwell Unveils 'Five Levels of Leadership,'" CBN News, January 9, 2012, http://www.cbn.com/cbnnews/finance/2012/January /John-Maxwell-Unveils-Five-Levels-of-Leadership/.

4. Interview with John Maxwell, January 7, 2013.

5. E-mail from Ryan Wall, April 17, 2013.

6. Bridges, *Managing Transitions*, 31.

7. Interview with John Maxwell, January 7, 2013.

8. E-mail from David and Jonathan Shibley, May 17, 2014.

9. Interview with John Maxwell, January 7, 2013.

10. Interview with Dave Stone, January 15, 2013.

11. Interview with John Maxwell, January 7, 2013.

12. Interview with Bob and Rob Hoskins, May 22, 2014.

13. Francis Chan, Leadership Network Succession Conference, March 26, 2013. All of the speakers from this conference were viewed via an online simulcast.

14. Interview with Lance Witt, February 19, 2013.

15. Interview with Larry Stockstill, March 13, 2013.

16. Stoyan Zaimov, "Rev. Robert Schuller 'Confused and Forgetful' in Testimony Against Crystal Cathedral," *Christian Post*, November 8, 2012, http://www.christianpost.com/news/rev-robert-schuller -confused-and-forgetful-in-testimony-against-crystal-cathedral-84648/.

17. Ibid.

18. Interview with John Maxwell, January 7, 2013.

19. William Vanderbloemen, Leadership Network Succession Conference, March 26, 2013.

Chapter 3

1. Jone Johnson Lewis, "Jackie Joyner-Kersee Quotes," About Women's History, http://womenshistory.about.com/od/quotes/a/joyner_kersee .htm, accessed June 18, 2014.

2. Drew Dyck, "War and Peace," *Leadership Journal*, October 24, 2011, http://www.christianitytoday.com/le/2011/fall/warpeace.html.

3. Bob Russell and Bryan Bucher, *Transition Plan* (Louisville: Minister's Label: 2010), 37.

4. *The History, by Herodotus: The Second Book, Entitled Euterpe*, available online at https://ebooks.adelaide.edu.au/h/herodotus/h4/book2.html.

5. William Bridges, *Managing Transitions: Making the Most of Change* (Philadelphia: Da Capo, 2009), 11.

6. Interview with Jonathan Bonar, October 12, 2012.

7. "Scheduled Passengers Carried," *IATA World Air Transport Statistics (WATS)*, 58th ed., http://www.iata.org/publications/pages/wats -passenger-carried.aspx, accessed July 29, 2014.

8. Jay Passavant, Leadership Network, March 26, 2013.

Chapter 4

1. John C. Maxwell, *Developing the Leaders Around You* (Nashville: Thomas Nelson, 1995), 22.
2. John Blake, "Two preaching giants and the 'betrayal' that tore them apart," CNN, November 19, 2012, http://www.cnn.com/2012/11/17 /us/andy-stanley/index.html.
3. Mother Teresa, ThinkExist.com, accessed August 12, 2014, http:// thinkexist.com/quotation/be_faithful_in_small_things_because_it_is_ in_them/14298.html.
4. Interview with John Maxwell, January 7, 2013.
5. See http://files.meetup.com/1459183/Everyone-Communicates -Workbook.pdf and http://www.iequip.org/download_file/view/519/.
6. Tom Mullins, *The Leadership Game: Seven Winning Principles from Eight National Champions* (Nashville, Thomas Nelson, 2005), 134.
7. E-mail from Todd Lane, June 4, 2014.
8. Larry Stockstill, *The Surge: A Global Church-Planting Initiative*, Kindle ed. (BookBaby, 2012), 57.
9. John Maxwell, *The 21 Indispensable Qualities of a Leader* (Nashville: Thomas Nelson, 1999), xi.

Chapter 5

1. Interview with Joel Osteen, February 19, 2013.
2. Interview with Jerry Falwell Jr., February 18, 2013.
3. Interview with Jonathan Falwell, February 26, 2013.
4. Interview with Joel Osteen.
5. Interview with Paul Osteen, February 19, 2013.
6. "Hillary Clinton: up to 27 million living in slavery," *Telegraph* (UK), June 20, 2012, http://www.telegraph.co.uk/news/worldnews /northamerica/usa/9343314/Hillary-Clinton-up-to-27-million-living -in-slavery.html.
7. National Human Trafficking Resource Center (NHTRC) 2013 Statistical Review, online at https://na4.salesforce.com/sfc /p/#300000006E4S/a/600000004U8X/g.ugT8Evt_r2. CrkWYkLzDMHDzjQBR1Qw9_1_yE1Kyg=.
8. Interview with Jerry Falwell Jr., February 18, 2013.
9. Interview with Jonathan Falwell, February 26, 2013.
10. Interview with Joel Osteen, February 19, 2013.
11. Interview with Rob Hoskins, May 22, 2014.
12. Interview with Dave Stone, January 15, 2013.
13. Interview with Larry Stockstill.

14. Mike Erre, Leadership Network Conference, March 26, 2013.
15. Interview with Jerry Falwell Jr., February 18, 2013.
16. Interview with Jonathan Falwell, February 26, 2013.
17. Charles Kettering, http://www.brainyquote.com/quotes/quotes/c /charlesket152037.html, accessed August 12, 2014.
18. Interview with Joel Osteen, February 19, 2013.
19. Jason Bolin, Leadership Network Conference, March 26, 2013.
20. Bryan Carter, Leadership Network Conference, March 26, 2013.
21. Gene Appel, Leadership Network Conference, March 26, 2013.
22. Interview with Jonathan Falwell, February 26, 2013.
23. Interview with Joel Osteen, February 19, 2013.
24. Adapted from *The Correspondence of Isaac Newton*, vol. 1, ed. H. W. Turnbull (published for the Royal Society at the University Press, 1959), 416.
25. Interview with John Maxwell, January 7, 2012.
26. Ibid.
27. Franklin D. Roosevelt, quoted at *Forbes.com*, accessed August 12, 2014, http://thoughts.forbes.com/thoughts/leadership-franklin-d-roosevelt -its-a-terrible.
28. Interview with Paul Osteen, February 19, 2013.
29. Interview with John Maxwell, January 7, 2012.

Chapter 6

1. John C. Maxwell, *Failing Forward: Turning Mistakes into Stepping Stones for Success* (Nashville: Thomas Nelson, 2000), 140.
2. Interview with John Maxwell, January 7, 2012.
3. E-mail from David Shibley, May 17, 2014.

Chapter 7

1. John C. Maxwell, *Failing Forward: Turning Mistakes into Stepping Stones for Success* (Nashville: Thomas Nelson, 2000), 81.
2. Jonathan Falwell, *One Great Truth: Finding Your Answers to Life* (New York: Howard Books, 2008), 1–9.
3. Interview with Jonathan Falwell, February 26, 2013.
4. Interview with Ross Parsley, February 19, 2013.
5. Interview with Jonathan Falwell, February 26, 2013.
6. Interview with Jerry Falwell Jr., February 18, 2013.
7. Interview with Paul Osteen, February 19, 2013.
8. Joel Osteen page, on the website of Lakewood Church (Houston, TX),

accessed July 2014, https://www.lakewoodchurch.com/pages/new
   -here/joel-osteen.aspx.

9. Interview with Bob and Rob Hoskins, May 22, 2014.
10. Interview with Jonathan Falwell, February 26, 2013.
11. Interview with Jerry Falwell Jr., February 18, 2013.
12. Personal conversation with Tuttle.
13. Interview with Jonathan Falwell, February 26, 2013.
14. Interview with Dan Southerland, March 5, 2013.
15. Jason Meyer, Leadership Network Conference, March 26, 2013.
16. Interview with Dan Southerland, March 5, 2013.
17. Mike Erre, Leadership Network Conference, March 26, 2013.
18. Interview with Dan Southerland, March 5, 2013.
19. Ibid.
20. Interview with Lance Witt, February 19, 2013.
21. Ross Parsley, *Messy Church: A Multigenerational Mission for God's
    Family* (Colorado Springs: David C. Cook, 2012), 167.
22. Interview with Lance Witt, February 19, 2013.
23. Jason Bolin, Leadership Network Conference, March 26, 2013.
24. Ibid.
25. Interview with Ross Parsley, February 19, 2013.
26. Interview with Dan Southerland, March 5, 2013.
27. Interview with Ross Parsley, February 19, 2013.
28. Interview with Dan Southerland, March 5, 2013.
29. Interview with Larry Stockstill, March 13, 2013.
30. Parsley, *Messy Church*, 186.
31. Interview with Dan Southerland, March 5, 2013.
32. Ibid.

Chapter 8

1. Wikiquote, s.v. "Pericles," http://en.wikiquote.org/wiki/Pericles,
   accessed August 1, 2014.
2. Marlene Baer, "Outrageous Hats and Sunday School," January 1, 2002,
   Christianity Today, http://www.christianitytoday.com/biblestudies
   /articles/churchhomeleadership/cr-2002-001-12.15.html.
3. www.cru.org/about/what-we-do/milestones, pp. 2–3.
4. Billy Graham Evangelistic Association, http://billygraham.org
   /biographies.
5. Ibid.
6. John C. Maxwell, *Real Leadership: The 101 Collection* (Nashville:
   Thomas Nelson, 2006).